The Impacts of Nanotechnology on Companies

POLICY INSIGHTS FROM CASE STUDIES

OECD

This work is published on the responsibility of the Secretary-General of the OECD. The opinions expressed and arguments employed herein do not necessarily reflect the official views of the Organisation or of the governments of its member countries.

Please cite this publication as:
OECD (2010), *The Impacts of Nanotechnology on Companies: Policy Insights from Case Studies,* OECD Publishing.
http://dx.doi.org/10.1787/9789264094635-en

ISBN 978-92-64-09462-8 (print)
ISBN 978-92-64-09463-5 (PDF)

Foreword

Nanotechnology is an emerging field and is currently receiving a good deal of attention in most industrialised countries, as large policy initiatives and related R&D investments demonstrate. It enables the purposeful engineering of matter at very small length scales – at the level of atoms and molecules – and can therefore contribute to new industrial applications in a very broad range of sectors. The fundamental characteristics of nanotechnology have led analysts to suggest that it may constitute a basis for long-term productivity and economic growth. It may also help to address pressing national and global challenges in areas such as health care, energy, water and climate change. Traditional science and technology indicators highlight the broad-based nature of nanotechnology, while consultants forecast large markets and contributions to entrepreneurship and job creation. Nonetheless, there is inadequate reliable information in terms of the implications of nanotechnology for companies and business environments and how policies for innovation should respond.

This report contributes to policy making by providing new information on the commercialisation of nanotechnology. It is based on a large number of company case studies assembled in order to assess whether nanotechnology is the source of new and specific challenges for companies which may require new types of policy responses. The project was carried out by the OECD Working Party on Nanotechnology (WPN), which was established in March 2007 to advise on emerging science, technology and innovation-related policy issues relating to the responsible development and use of nanotechnology. The project has relied on the active participation of a large number of WPN delegates and has drawn on a workshop hosted by Finland in Helsinki in October 2008 to discuss preliminary findings.

The lead countries for the project were Canada and Switzerland, and the OECD Secretariat would like in particular to thank Vanessa Clive and Marsha Permut at Industry Canada, and Rachel Grange from the École Polytechnique Fédérale de Lausanne, Switzerland for their leadership and contribution throughout. The contributions of participating companies in the form of their valuable expertise and time were essential to the success of this project and are gratefully acknowledged. The analysis of the case studies and the preparation of this report were undertaken by Christopher Palmberg, with inputs from Jacqueline Allan and Kate Le Strange, all at the OECD Directorate for Science, Technology and Industry.

Table of contents

Figures

Tables

Executive summary

Nanotechnology is an emerging technology (or set of technologies) which is currently attracting wide-ranging attention. Almost no other field has obtained as much public investment in R&D in a such a short time, and private-sector investments have also increased steadily (there is as yet no reliable systematic data revealing how the economic crisis may have affected this). Consultancies predict very large markets for nanotechnology-enabled products, and forecasts suggest that many new jobs may be created. To describe the potential economic impact of nanotechnology, reference is often made to the concept of "general purpose technology", that is, a technology with a range of characteristics which makes it particularly well placed to generate longer-term productivity increases and economic growth across a range of industries. As a consequence, governments are developing strategies to promote the responsible development and use of nanotechnology while taking account of the uncertainties and any risks involved.

However, there is a lack of comprehensive, internationally comparable information on how different types of companies are affected by nano-technology, how they use it in their innovative activities, how they acquire or develop relevant competences, as well as on the specific commercialisation challenges they face. There is also uncertainty about the different role that new and small as well as larger companies will play in the commercialisation of nanotechnology. This report, based on 51 company case studies, seeks to help to fill that gap, to add to previous studies and to suggest areas for future work. The case studies are drawn from 17 countries and cover a range of company sizes, nanotechnology sub-areas and fields of application. They provide qualitative insights into the commercialisation of nanotechnology from the viewpoint of companies and thus complement studies which have relied primarily on publication and patent data or statistical surveys. The question which the case studies have mainly addressed is whether new and specific challenges arise during the development and commercialisation of nanotechnology which may require new types of policy responses. However, as nanotechnology covers a broad range of sub-areas, fields of application and research/engineering approaches it has sometimes been difficult to single out challenges which are truly specific to nanotechnology. Moreover, the findings may not necessarily apply to all sub-areas and application fields.

Nanotechnology has its basis in the converging application of physics, chemistry and biology to using the new properties of materials and systems that emerge below the 100 nanometre length scale. Its emergence has been spurred by key inventions in instrumentation and further supported by significant policy initiatives in most developed countries, involving, among other things, sizeable R&D funding, the founding of new research centres and new agencies. The scattered analyses of the impact of nanotechnology on companies and business environments which have been undertaken highlight its interdisciplinary, science-based and market-driven nature. Statistical surveys point to challenges such as bottlenecks in funding and human resources and the poor process scalability of R&D. Intellectual property rights (IPR) issues and public perception of nanotechnology can also complicate the business environment. These earlier studies provide a useful backdrop for the case studies discussed in this report. Some of its findings reinforce, and deepen, those of previous studies while others raise new issues. The main findings are of this study are:

- Nanotechnology is an enabling technology (or set of technologies) and the company case studies show that this feature is a major reason for their entry into the field. Nanotechnology allows for both the improvement of existing and the development of completely new products and processes, and sometimes new services as well. Companies often experiment with multiple applications at the same time, many of which are still in the research phase.

- Nanotechnology may best be described as a "science-based and demand-driven field". While all of the case study companies undertake in-house R&D, collaboration with universities and "star scientists" are also important sources of innovation and knowledge, especially for small companies. Larger companies in relatively mature nanotechnology sub-areas appear to focus more on applications which are driven by market demand and tend to collaborate with a broader range of organisations to leverage their in-house R&D.

- Nanotechnology mainly affects the R&D and production activities of the case study companies. Many of the smaller companies focus exclusively on nanotechnology, while the larger ones typically blend nanotechnology with a range of other technologies. In the larger companies it is thus difficult to single out the share of nanotechnology in total labour costs, R&D expenditure, production costs, capital spending and sales.

- The larger companies in the sample have typically been involved in nanotechnology for many years and seem well placed to assimilate nanotechnology due to their established critical mass in R&D and production, their ability to acquire and operate expensive instrumentation and to access and use external knowledge. The relative strength of larger companies in the early phases of nanotechnology developments runs counter to what the traditional model of company dynamics and technology lifecycles would predict where smaller, younger companies are generally considered more innovative.

- The case studies illustrate that nanotechnology is a complex field owing to its dependency on various scientific disciplines, research/engineering approaches and advanced instrumentation. Further, many nanotechnology sub-areas are in an early, immature, phase of development. These features of nanotechnology can often create barriers to entry especially for smaller companies which have limited human and other resources. They also contribute to the poor process scalability of nanoscale engineering during the transition from R&D to pilot and industrial scale production.

- Difficulties arise for recruiting human resources, especially for R&D and production activities. The need for employees, or so-called gatekeepers, who combine specialist and general knowledge (knowledge integration) and can manage interdisciplinary teams is also a challenge.

- Challenges to funding R&D and related activities are often mentioned, especially by business start-ups. The poor process scalability of R&D, which raises costs and prolongs new product development times, can make nanotechnology less attractive to investors. Uncertain regulatory environments and public perceptions of nanotechnology's environmental, health and safety (EHS) risks can also influence R&D funding.

- The novelty of nanotechnology, the established interests of stakeholders, and difficulties that companies can have in communicating the value proposition of applications to potential customers (*e.g.* other companies), makes their entry and positioning in value chains harder. The challenge is even greater for smaller companies that experiment with multiple applications and have to monitor many different industries and business environments.

- Intellectual property rights (IPR) may become an issue as commercialisation progresses and nanotechnology matures as there is already a very wide range of patent claims, and the possible formation of patent thickets (interrelated and overlapping patents), which could contribute to barriers to entry for companies.

- The potential for overreaction to both actual and perceived EHS uncertainties and risks, combined with regulatory uncertainties, complicates the business environment for companies. Global harmonisation of future EHS regulations is considered important.

- These findings raise a range of policy challenges. The limitations of a case study approach should be borne in mind, however, when drawing implications, particularly regarding specific nanotechnology sub-areas and fields of application. Some of the challenges identified may lie outside the scope of policy, while others may only apply to certain countries and regions of the world. For example, the framework conditions for nanotechnology in less developed countries may be quite different from those in the developed countries from which the company case studies derive. With these limitations in mind, the following policy issues have been identified:

  i) Nanotechnology is a multifaceted technology that covers a broad range of sub-areas, fields of application and research/engineering approaches; it does not share the characteristics of a specific "industry". As a consequence, a general "nanotechnology policy" may not be appropriate. **Strategies and policy instruments need to be tailored to the specific sub-areas and application fields in which nanotechnology evolves, while also acknowledging the multiplicity of research/engineering approaches.**

  ii) Companies cannot easily single out the impacts of nanotechnology on their activities, sales and revenues, especially larger companies which blend nanotechnology with a range of other technologies. It is therefore difficult to define, identify and monitor company activities in this field. **New types of indicators are needed along with jointly agreed definitions to effectively monitor the developing use of nanotechnology. Qualitative case study work will remain important as the field develops.**

  iii) The innovation literature has identified the strong role of start-ups in the development and commercialisation of new technologies. However, this received wisdom may not apply fully to nanotechnology. While start-ups play an important role, larger and established companies seem to be relatively well positioned to use and develop nanotechnology owing to their ability to acquire and run expensive instrumentation, R&D and production activities, and to their established, broad technological knowledge base. Accordingly, **policy should also address larger and established companies as well as start-ups.**

  iv) Commercialisation raises many challenges. This report highlights some which are relatively specific to nanotechnology whereas others are common to offer high-technology areas such as biotechnology. Some of them apply more to start-ups while others apply more to medium-sized or large companies. **It is important to recognise that such challenges are often related.** For example, those relating to

R&D often also concern human resources and manufacturing issues. EHS concerns feed back into R&D strategies, and problems in securing funding may also have to do with technical barriers during R&D. **Policy should acknowledge the different challenges facing companies of different sizes, and note the importance of co-ordination of different agencies and instruments. In effect, policies for innovation need to display coherence.**

v) The poor process scalability of R&D, *i.e.* challenges in the transition from R&D to pilot and industrial scale production, is among the most pervasive challenges identified in the case study sample. This may be due to the early phase of many nanotechnology sub-areas and constitutes a barrier to entry into established value chains and to the commercialisation of nanotechnology. This suggests that **policies should recognise the importance both of manufacturing techno-logies and product development, as well as supportive infra-structure (instrumentation, clean rooms, centres of excellence, etc.).**

vi) Companies face human resource constraints. They need to identify and recruit both specialists and generalists who can act as gate-keepers across scientific disciplines, organisational boundaries and various engineering approaches. The management of interdisci-plinary teams and the integration of different strands of knowledge also present challenges. **Policy should therefore be attentive to the education of specialists and generalists and should facilitate interdisciplinary collaboration and vocational training in nano-scale manufacturing.**

vii) Start-up companies in particular face challenges to entering established value chains. The entry barriers identified include poor process scalability of R&D, technical uncertainties and the multiplicity of potential applications, along with issues relating to communicating the value proposition of nanotechnology-enabled applications. **Policies should recognise these entry barriers for start-ups and facilitate linkages between dedicated start-ups and large and established companies, while also promoting the involvement of medium-sized companies.**

viii) There are explicit challenges relating to the funding of R&D and to IPR, in particular overly broad patent claims, the emergence of patent thickets, or, indeed, inadequate valuation of intellectual assets. **Policies should pay attention to possible IPR-related challenges and funding constraints related to nanotechnology start-ups as the field develops, especially if the lack of venture capital available to the sector continues.**

ix) Finally, the case study companies expressed concern about regulatory uncertainties regarding EHS issues and public perceptions of the related risks. These issues affect the types of R&D projects and business opportunities which companies pursue. The sectoral specificities of EHS risks should be identified and better understood. **Policies should support the development of transparent, timely and tailored guidelines for assessing EHS risks to cover different types of nanotechnology sub-areas and fields of application, while also striving for further international harmonisation.**

The company case studies reported here, along with the earlier studies to which this report refers, provide a good basis for further analytical work on the responsible development and use of nanotechnology. The findings highlight a broad range of challenges for commercialisation of nanotechnology which should be explored in greater detail and in the context of specific nanotechnology sub-areas and fields of application. Some of the challenges will become clearer once nanotechnology starts to enter markets in a more visible way. Further policy co-ordination and better, and internationally comparable, intelligence on the business environments impacting on companies commercialising nanotechnology is essential for unlocking its full potential.

Chapter 1

Introduction:
The definitions, development and
possible economic impacts of nanotechnology

Owing to its inherent characteristics, nanotechnology may play an important role in upgrading traditional industries by enabling new functionalities and adding value to existing products. Nanotechnology can also enable more radical innovation and thus the growth of new companies and industries, especially if it converges with other technology fields such as biotechnology and ICT.

Background

As an emerging technology, nanotechnology has attracted worldwide attention. It has been estimated that global R&D investments in nanotechnology amounted to approximately USD 13.5 billion in 2007 with public investments accounting for roughly half of this total. The most optimistic consultancy estimates forecast that the global value of products incorporating nanotechnology will range from USD 1 trillion to as much as USD 3.1 trillion by 2015. At the high end, this has been predicted to lead to some 2 million new jobs worldwide. These forecasts may be significantly inflated owing to methodological problems for measuring nanotechnology and will also have to be adjusted in view of the impact of the economic crisis. Nonetheless, nanotechnology is likely to remain at the top of policy agendas as countries start to look beyond the crisis and engage with emerging technologies for competitiveness and long-term economic growth.

Nanotechnology is frequently referred to as the new "general purpose technology" of the 21st century, following earlier technologies which have been a springboard for long-term productivity increases and economic growth (the prime recent example is information and communication technology [ICT], particularly computers). A general purpose technology is one that develops rapidly in terms of its ability to offer new functionalities and better performance in existing products and processes. It has different uses in a broad range of industries and promotes structural and organisational changes in terms of business models and company and industry dynamics (see Box 1.1). Owing to its inherent characteristics, nanotechnology may play an important role in upgrading traditional industries by enabling new functionalities and adding value to existing products. Nanotechnology can also enable more radical innovation and thus the growth of new companies and industries, especially if it converges with other technology fields such as biotechnology and ICT.

Nanotechnology holds out the promise of strong economic potential and may also help to address global challenges such as those relating to climate change, affordable health care, access to clean water, energy and other resource constraints. However, unlocking this potential will require balanced and co-ordinated policy responses. These must also take into account the uncertainties and risks involved, as nanotechnology is likely to disrupt the knowledge base of existing companies and industries. It also introduces concerns about environmental, health and safety (EHS) and ethical, legal and societal (ELS) issues. Against this backdrop, governments are now weighing suitable policy approaches and considering broader socio-economic implications and risks. However, they lack comprehensive and internationally comparable analyses of how nanotechnology affects companies and business environments.

Box 1.1. Characteristics of a general purpose technology

1. It should provide *rapid and significant scope for improvements over existing technologies in economic terms*. This reflects the performance of some function that is vital to the functioning of a large segment of existing or potential products and production systems. For example, "continuous rotary motion" and "binary logic" can be considered to embody these characteristics in steam power and ICT, respectively, as key examples of previous general purpose technologies.

2. It should have a *widening variety of uses in a widening number of application areas and industries*. This reflects the enabling and generic nature of general purpose technologies which supports its widespread adoption throughout industries and economies. Widespread adoption may not only be a consequence of the scope of improvements related to a technology, it also relates to a variety of actors, and to beliefs about the promise of the technology.

3. It should both *generate, and depend on, the development of a range of complementary technologies or innovations*. These technologies and innovations may relate not only to supporting production methods, components and other intermediaries. They may also relate to new organisations of companies and industries, different types of business models or changes in the overall business environment of companies.

Source: Based on Helpman (1998); Lipsey *et al.* (2005).

Until now nanotechnology developments have mainly been analysed through data on R&D expenditures, publications and patents, as well as company surveys in a few countries (*e.g.* Noyons *et al.*, 2003; Heinze, 2004; Huang *et al.*, 2004; OECD, 2007; Hullmann, 2007; Li *et al.*, 2007; NCMS and NSF, 2006; Malanowski *et al.*, 2006; Dandolopartners, 2006; and McNiven, 2007). While these studies provide important insights, they do not reveal the underlying drivers for companies' involvement and the specific challenges they face during R&D, production, commercialisation and marketing. By and large there are only a few in-depth case studies that highlight specific issues which are of direct concern to companies and may require policy attention. As both private and public R&D investments continue to grow, and as the potential breadth and impact of nanotechnology applications become clearer, it is increasingly urgent for policy makers to gain more insights into these issues.

Definitions of nanotechnology

Various agencies have proposed definitions of nanotechnology for planning and implementing policies and initiatives in the field. However, no commonly agreed international framework yet exists; the International Organization for Standardization (ISO) is engaged in this task. The OECD is also considering definitions for statistical work. But such international harmonisation of definitions remains a work in progress. Therefore, this report has to rely on a set of general policy-related definitions which are found in various government reports and policy documents.

Table 1.1 lists the definitions used by the United States (US), the European Union (EU) and Japan, the main countries/regions in terms of public investments in nanotechnology R&D. It also includes the so-called "scoping definition" under development by ISO, which constitutes the framework for the definition of nanotechnology of the OECD Working Party on Nanotechnology (WPN), and the definition used by the European Patent Office (EPO), the main source for internationally comparable patent data on nanotechnology.

While the wording of these definitions differs, all refer to three common aspects of nanotechnology. First, nanotechnology is considered to involve the purposeful "control", "manipulation" or "handling" of matter at a very small scale. This is intended to eliminate from the definition any material or process that has come about through "accidental" nanotechnology, *i.e.* nano-technology that occurs naturally or has occurred without purposeful engineering. The techniques for producing the coloured stained glass windows of medieval churches by using the optical properties of nano-sized gold particles would be an example of accidental nanotechnology. In modern times synthetic zeolites, primarily used to make detergents, catalyse petro-chemical processes and serve as desiccants, have been "accidentally" manu-factured through nanotechnology processes. There are also numerous examples of nanotechnology in nature.

Table 1.1. Common nanotechnology definitions

Source	Definition
US: National Nanotechnology Initiative (2001-)	Nanotechnology is the understanding and control of matter at dimensions of roughly 1 to 100 nanometres, where unique phenomena enable novel applications. Encompassing nanoscale science, engineering and technology, nanotechnology involves imaging, measuring, modelling, and manipulating matter at this length scale.
EU: 7th Framework Programme (2007-2013)	Generating new knowledge on interface and size-dependent phenomena; nano-scale control of material properties for new applications; integration of technologies at the nano-scale; self-assembling properties; nano-motors; machines and systems; methods and tools for characterisation and manipulation at nano dimensions; nano precision technologies in chemistry for the manufacture of basic materials and components; impact on human safety, health and the environment; metrology, monitoring and sensing, nomenclature and standards; exploration of new concepts and approaches for sectoral applications, including the integration and convergence of emerging technologies.
Japan: Second Science and Technology Basic Plan (2001-05)	Nanotechnology is an interdisciplinary S&T that encompasses IT technology, the environmental sciences, life sciences, materials science, etc. It is for controlling and handling atoms and molecules in the order of nano (1/1 000 000 000) meter enabling discovery of new functions by taking advantage of its material characteristics unique to nano size, so that it can bring technological innovation in various fields.
Working definition of ISO in 2007	Understanding and control of matter and processes at the nanoscale, typically, but not exclusively, below 100 nanometres in one or more dimensions where the onset of size-dependent phenomena usually enables novel applications. Utilising the properties of nanoscale materials that differ from the properties of individual atoms, molecules, and bulk matter, to create improved materials, devices, and systems that exploit these new properties.
European Patent Office (EPO) in 2009	The term nanotechnology covers entities with a geometrical size of at least one functional component below 100 nanometres in one or more dimensions susceptible of making physical, chemical or biological effects available which are intrinsic to that size. It covers equipment and methods for controlled analysis, manipulation, processing, fabrication or measurement with a precision below 100 nanometres.

The second common aspect of these definitions is the emphasis on a particular measurement scale, whereby research and engineering move into the nanotechnology domain by reason of the onset of size-dependent phenomena due to substantial increases in surface area or other effects that only emerge at the nanoscale. In the US, ISO and EPO definitions, a threshold of 100 nanometres is suggested for the onset of such size-dependent phenomena. In practice this threshold is not fixed, as size-dependent phenomena emerge along a continuum that can extend above 100 nanometres. It is merely indicative of a point at which the classical rules of physics start to give way to quantum mechanical effects and the related new, and so far less well known, phenomena that nanotechnology relies on in important ways.

The third aspect of the definitions is the most critical from the viewpoint of commercialisation. It is that nanotechnology enables "novel" or "new" industrial applications or "technological innovations". This feature has led some analysts to call nanotechnology the next general purpose technology, as discussed above. For example, the EU definition emphasises the integration of technologies at the nanoscale, highlights various areas of application and stresses the characteristic of nanotechnology in the context of the "integration and convergence of emerging technologies". The Japanese definition proposes that nanotechnology can "bring technological innovation in various fields". The convergent nature of nanotechnology is also often highlighted. It refers to the commonly held belief that the possibility to use the same/similar basic building blocks (*e.g.* atoms and molecules) and tools of analysis (microscopy, high-capacity computers, etc.) across various scientific disciplines will lead to the partial fusion of nanotechnology, biotechnology, information technology and cognitive sciences (sometimes referred to as NBIC) (Roco, 2007).

On closer examination it is also clear that many policy papers use both single definitions of nanotechnology, like those above, and so-called list-based definitions. These are lists of science and technology areas that are considered to fall under the term nanotechnology. Single-based definitions may be useful for building consensus and defining overall policy strategies. List-based definitions may be more relevant for companies involved in the technology and industrial areas in which nanotechnology can be applied. Table 1.2 provides one list-based definition of nanotechnology, developed by the EPO. This definition will be the basis for displaying patent data and results from the company case studies later in the report.

Table 1.2. List-based definition of nanotechnology

Title	Examples
Nanobiotechnology	Nanocapsules as carriers for therapy and pharmaceutical treatment. Biomolecular motors Molecular arrangements for biocatalysts Pre-targeting with peptides or antibodies Host-guest complexes or radioactive pharmaceutical preparations
Nanoelectronics	DNA computing Quantum computing Single electron logic Nanotube displays Biomolecules for electronic and data storage Read heads with nm precision
Nanomaterials	Nanoparticles, composites, dendrinmes, nanotubes and fullerenes Supramolecular systems Ultrathin functional films Self-assembling monolayers (SAM) Hydrogen storage in nanostructured materials
Instruments	Measurement of physical, chemical, biological properties at surfaces with nm resolution Measurement of interfaces with lateral resolutions in the nm-range Normalisation routines for nanoanalytics Measurement of size distribution of nanoparticles Tools for ultra-precision engineering Use of quantum dot labels for analysing biological material
Nano-optics	Optical quantum well structures Photonic crystals Quantum optics Optical surfaces with nm surface prevision
Nanomagnetics	Low dimensional magnetism XMR technologies such as magnetoimpedance, anisotropic magnetoresistance, tunnelling magnetoresistance

Source: Scheu *et al.* (2006).

The origin and development of nanotechnology

In 1959, attention was first drawn to the importance of what was later defined as "nanotechnology" by the physicist Richard Feynman in a seminal talk at the meeting of the American Physical Society at the Californian Institute of Technology entitled "There's plenty of room at the bottom". He anticipated the possibility of controlling matter at a very small scale and thus introduced the scientific community to a new field of enquiry. The term "nanotechnology" was first used in 1974 by Norio Tangichi of the Tokyo University of Science, and the basic idea was explored in greater detail by Eric Drexler in his much-cited book *Engines of Creation – The Coming Era of Nanotechnology*.

However, the main impetus for nanotechnology developments came from certain key inventions in the field of instrumentation during the 1980s. A first milestone was the invention in 1981 of the Scanning Tunnelling Microscope (STM) by Gerd Binning and Heinrich Rohrer at the IBM Research Laboratory in Zurich, Switzerland. The STM enables atomic-scale imaging of surfaces that could not previously be achieved. The range of materials that could be characterised increased further with the invention in 1986 of the Atomic Force Microscope (AFM), again by Gerd Binning and his colleagues at IBM. The significance of these inventions was recognised by the Nobel Prize for Physics in 1986.

Since then, nanotechnology has taken important steps forward. However, examination and analysis of developments in nanotechnology are hampered by the absence of common definitions and statistical frameworks and thus by a lack of data. Publication and patent data are currently the only internationally comparable data available. They are relevant for this emerging and rapidly developing field because they are available as very detailed, relatively timely, and lengthy time series. Extensive analysis of nanotechnology publications and patenting was undertaken by the WPN (OECD, 2009) and forms the basis for some of the figures referred to below.

Nanotechnology patenting started to increase rapidly some 10-15 years after the key inventions in instrumentation (STM, AFM) in the 1980s (see Figure 1.1). A similar trend is found in biotechnology, where growth in patenting followed the invention of recombinant DNA and related techniques in the early 1970s (Zucker and Darby, 2005; Kaiser, 2006). A few high-profile discoveries may have brought the term "nanotechnology" into the foreground and then set its use, thereby encouraging researchers and inventors from adjacent areas to begin to work on "nanotechnology" topics. Nanotechnology and biotechnology patenting are currently both growing at a rate that clearly exceeds that of patenting in general (see OECD, 2009).

Figure 1.1. Nanotechnology patenting

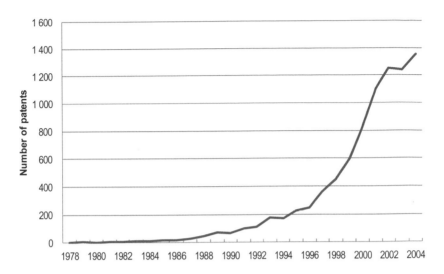

Note: The data are based on nanotechnology keyword searches in the European patent Office (patent) databases. Patents refer to Euro-PCT applications; data truncation after 2004 due to lags in the publishing of patents.

Source: OECD patent database, January 2008.

More recent advances include new nanotechnology-engineered materials (*e.g.* quantum dots, fullerenes or "buckyballs", and carbon nanotubes) and a range of new and improved instrumentation and other tools. The new materials can be used in a wide range of applications to enhance existing products and processes or create new ones and have also fuelled the rapid growth in patenting. For example, carbon nanotubes are a new class of carbon materials at the nanoscale with novel chemical, physical and electrical properties. They are mechanically very strong but also flexible and conduct electricity extremely well. Applications are to be found in solar cells, coatings, sports equipment, memory chips, etc. While nanomaterials only constitute one sub-area of the broader field of nanotechnology, they play an important role as platforms for many different types of applications.

Box 1.2. Nanotechnology development milestones

1959	Nobel prize winner in physics Robert Feynman's "There's plenty of room at the bottom"
1966	Quantum confinement effect discovered by Alan Fowler and colleagues at IBM
1974	"Nanotechnology" concept proposed by Norio Taniguchi of the Tokyo University of Science
1981	STM invented by Gerd Binning and Heinrich Rohrer of IBM, US
1982	Quantum dot, laser application proposed by Yasuhiko Arakawa and Hiroyuki Sakaki of the University of Tokyo
1984	Fullerene discovered by Richard Smilley and colleagues of Rice University in the United States
1986	AFM invented by Gerd Binning and colleagues at IBM
1986	Eric Drexler of MIT in the United States publishes *Engines of Creation: The Coming Era of Nanotechnology*
1986	Foresight Nanotech Institute established as the first one to educate society about the benefits and risks
1987	First commercial STM shipped by Digital Instruments in the United States
1989	First commercial AFM shipped by Digital Instruments in the United States
1990	The IBM logo produced with individual atoms for promotional reasons
1991	Carbon nanotubes discovered by Sumio Ijima of NEC, Japan
1991	AFM used on living cells stimulated the cross-pollination of nanotechnology and biotechnology
1990s	China adds nanotechnology to its S&T priorities in the 863 National High Technology Programme at MOST
1999	Discovery of dip-pen nanolithography by Chad Mirkin at Northwestern University in the United States
2000	The Centre for Nanotechnologies at the Chinese Academy of Sciences opens in Beijing
2001	National Nanotechnology Initiative launched in the United States
2002	Nanotechnology Research Network Centre of Japan established
2002	The European Commission designated nanotechnology a priority area in the Sixth Framework Programme
2003	A report by Greenpeace acknowledges both the risks and environmental benefits of nanotechnology
2004	The "21st Century Nanotechnology Research and Development Act" enacted in the United States provides further funding
2005	The Japanese "Strategic Technology Roadmap" published
2006	The 3rd Science and Technology Basic Plan launched in Japan
2006	The EU "Roadmaps at 2015 on Nanotechnology Application" published
2007	Russia announces a USD 8 billion investment in nanotechnology for 2007-15
2008	The US "Technology Roadmap for Productive Nanosystems" published
2008	Korean "Nanotechnology Roadmap" published

Sources: True Nano, Kaiser (2006), various websites.

The policy attention enjoyed by nanotechnology largely began with the establishment in 2001 of the National Nanotechnology Initiative (NNI) in the United States (see Box 1.2). The NNI was soon followed by extensive nanotechnology initiatives in Japan and several other countries, as well as in the EU. In Japan, nanotechnology was highlighted in the second Science and Technology Basic Plan 2001-05, and further emphasised in the third plan launched in 2006. In the EU, nanotechnology was designated a priority area in the Sixth Framework Programme for Research and Technological Development, initiated in 2002. The European Commission adopted the "Communication towards a European Strategy for Nanotechnology" in 2004, and in 2005, based on subsequent consultations, launched "Nanosciences and Nanotechnologies: An Action Plan for Europe 2005-2009". Nanotechnology is also included in the EU Seventh Framework Programme for 2007-2013.

The term "nanotechnology" is now commonly used, but the degree to which it describes a new scientific and technological area or merely relabels existing research agendas is still debated. This is an important issue as unrealistic expectations about the economic significance of new technologies can lead to financial bubbles and backlashes with adverse effects for their further development (Perez, 2002). Relabeling also complicates the R&D funding landscape for both public- and private-sector actors. The conceptual debate about nanotechnology is thus an important one and will continue. This report takes as a point of departure a few fundamental facts that highlight some of the novel and specific aspects of nanotechnology.

As noted, nanotechnology has emerged from the convergence of various subfields in physics, biology and chemistry and the joint realisation of new research and engineering opportunities at the nanoscale. A distinction is often made between the so-called "top-down" and "bottom-up" approaches to nanoscale engineering (see Figure 1.2). The "top-down" approach is essentially an incremental continuation of R&D trajectories in physics. It manipulates materials down to the nanoscale through more elaborate lithography, cutting, etching and grinding techniques.

Figure 1.2. Two main approaches to nanoscale engineering

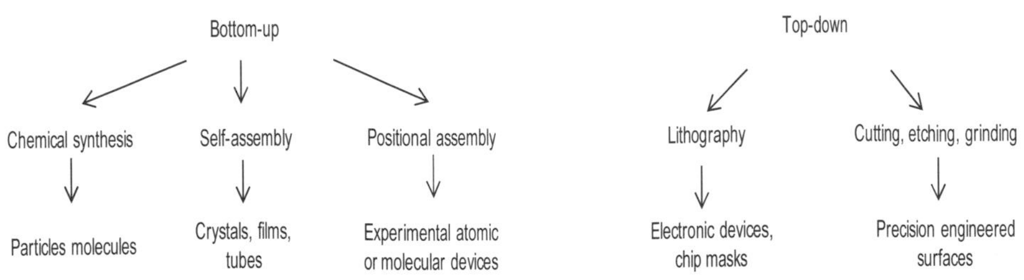

Source: The Royal Society (2004).

The "bottom-up" approach, instead, creates new materials at the nanoscale, for example through chemical synthesis, self-assembly and positional assembly. It can involve the controlled self-assembly of molecules and their macrostructures, based on the manipulation of individual atoms, and also draws on biotechnology. The top-down approach is currently more common, especially owing to its applications in the electronics industry. The bottom-up approach still faces many bottlenecks, especially when considering the cost-efficient scaling of some of the techniques for industrial use, as well as EHS and ELS concerns. Some of the more optimistic visions of what nanotechnology can do are inspired by bottom-up approaches (Hall, 2005).

As mentioned, the main impetus for nanotechnology developments came from certain key inventions in instrumentation, such as the STM and AFM, during the 1980s. The economic significance of these inventions stemmed from the fact that they enabled the characterisation of materials at the nanoscale through relatively routine procedures, and thus contributed to the worldwide diffusion of basic nanotechnology techniques. Even though nanotechnology has already produced applications and is entering industries and markets through these applications, it still is in a very early phase of development and so far lacks clearly defined commercial breakthroughs. It is essentially a broad term which describes a range of research and engineering approaches on the nanoscale. Accordingly, it is important to consider definitions of nanotechnology in some greater detail.

Possible economic impacts of nanotechnology

Patenting

Although nanotechnology is still in an early phase of development, it follows various trajectories towards many industrial uses and also appears to be cross-pollinating with other enabling technologies such as biotechnology and ICT. These trends are also visible in patenting across nanotechnology sub-areas and fields of application, particularly in nanoelectronics and nanomaterials. The primary intended fields of application of these patents are electronics, instruments and chemicals, followed by pharmaceuticals and industrial processing. Figure 1.3 displays the distribution of patents by nanotechnology sub-areas and fields of application.

Figure 1.3. Patenting by nanotechnology sub-areas and fields of application

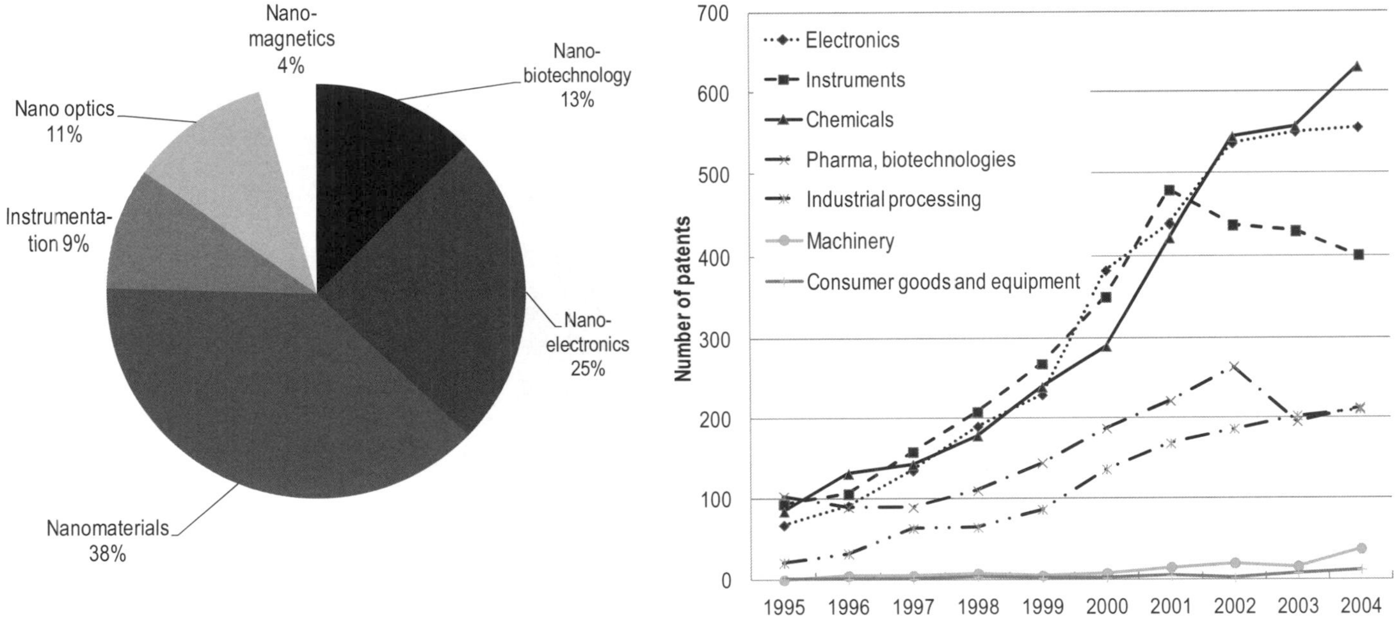

Note: These data refer to Euro-PCT applications.

Source: OECD patent database, January 2008.

The rapid growth of nanotechnology-related patenting in information technology and semiconductors is in line with sectoral roadmaps commissioned in this industry regarding the possibilities offered by the top-down approach to nanoscale engineering (see especially the International Technology Roadmap for Semiconductors; *www.itrs.net*). It is believed that nanotechnology may ensure further capacity increases in microprocessors. Reference is commonly made to "Moore's Law", which predicts a doubling approximately every two years of the number of transistors that can be placed on an integrated circuit, a phenomenon which has underpinned the rapid development of the semiconductor industry. Nanotechnology can contribute by enabling the scaling down of the size of transistors to nanometre lengths. It can also create new materials with extraordinary conductivity to replace the materials traditionally used in the manufacturing of transistors.

The bottom-up approach to nanoscale engineering is likely to be more discontinuous and science-based. Bottom-up approaches may require more interdisciplinary collaboration between physics, chemistry and biology (including biotechnology). While it may be too early to suggest that inter-disciplinary collaboration is leading to the convergence of nanotechnology, biotechnology, information technology and cognitive sciences (NBIC), bottom-up approaches may give rise to some unexpected applications in the short run.

Products and applications

Very little is known so far about how companies are applying nanotechnology for innovation and the development of new processes and products. Some indications can be gained from a recent nanotechnology product inventory by the Project on Emerging Nanotechnologies at the Woodrow Wilson International Centre for Scholars in the United States (see *www.nanotechproject.org*). Product listings for this inventory were compiled through web-based searches using three selection criteria: products that can be readily purchased by consumers, that can be identified as nanotechnology-based by the manufacturer or another source, and for which the nano-technology-based claims appear reasonable.

In August 2009 the inventory contained a total of 1015 nanotechnology products or product lines, up substantially from 212 in 2006. Figure 1.4 displays the distribution of these products by category (left-hand chart) and by region (right-hand chart). US companies dominate with a total of 540 products, followed by East Asian countries (China, Chinese Taipei, Korea and Japan) with 240 and Europe (United Kingdom, France, Germany, Finland, Switzerland, Italy and Sweden) with 154.

Figure 1.4. Nanotechnology products by main category and region of origin (2009)

By category

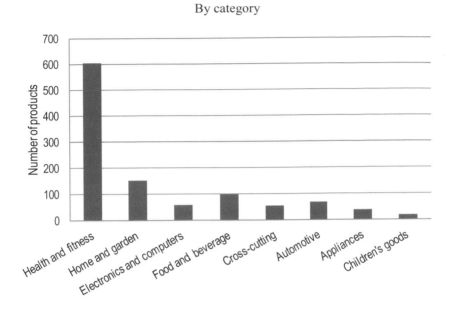

By region of origin

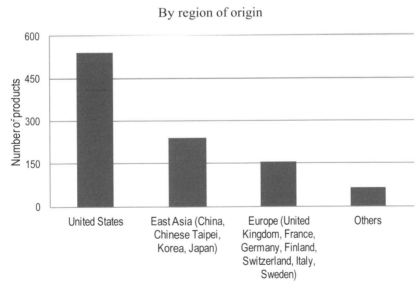

Source: www.nanotechproject.org/inventories/consumer/.

Box 1.3. Examples of nanotechnology applications

Electronics and communications

Data storage media with very high recording densities, new flat-panel plastic display technologies, new materials for semiconductors that increase processing speeds, the realisation of molecular or biomolecular electronics, spintronics and quantum computing.

Materials and construction

Use of nanoparticles and coatings for reinforced materials and machinery parts, super-hard and tough drill bits and cutting tools, "smart" magnetic fluids for vacuum seals and lubricants, scratch-proof or non-wettable surfaces, anti-bacterial construction material, self-cleaning and reactive eco-efficient windows.

Pharmaceuticals and health care

Potential applications include miniaturised diagnostics that can be implanted for the early diagnosis and monitoring of illnesses, nanoscale coatings to improve the bioactivity and biocompatibility of implants, ultra-precise nanostructured drug delivery systems, sensors for labs-on-a-chip, new materials for bone and tissue regeneration.

Machinery and tools

Nanopowders sintered into bulk materials to give special properties, extremely sensitive sensors to detect incipient failures and actuators to repair problems, chemical-mechanical polishing with nanoparticles, self-assembly of structures from molecules, bio-inspired materials and biostructures.

Energy

New types of batteries, artificial photosynthesis for clean energy, efficient low-cost photovoltaic solar cells (*e.g.* solar "paint"), safe storage of hydrogen for use as a clean fuel.

Environment and water

Enhanced membranes for water purification, nanostructured filters for removing pollutants from industrial effluents, improved remediation methods (*e.g.* photo-catalytic techniques).

Source: OECD (2005, 2009) and various others.

The categorisation of nanotechnology products shows that they are concentrated in the fields of health and fitness. The largest sub-categories are cosmetics, clothing, personal care and sporting equipment. The remaining products are relatively evenly distributed across the main categories of home and garden, electronics and computers, food and beverages, cross-cutting (*e.g.* multiple use), automotive, appliances, and children's goods. However, it should be strongly emphasised that this database is restricted to consumer products whereby no conclusions can be made about the relative significance of consumer and non-consumer (*e.g.* business to business intermediate products) in the commercialising of nanotechnology. Nanotechnology is, perhaps above all, potentially enabling a broad range of less visible intermediate products applications (see Box 1.3

for some examples). Many of these applications are business-to-business products or intermediate inputs to products or systems. Other limitations of the data should also be borne in mind, such as the absence of clear-cut definitions and an unclear sampling frame, and the fact that the propensity to publish these products on the Internet may be due to many different factors. The limitations of the data are also highlighted by the Woodrow Wilson International Centre for Scholars.

Market growth and jobs

The degree to which nanotechnology applications and products will affect economies in a broader sense is still very hard to assess. Thus far, forecasts by consultancies and some commercial banks have led in predicting economic impacts from the perspective of market volumes for nanotechnology-enabled products. Overall the forecasts vary significantly owing to the use of different methodologies, but all suggest very rapid growth in the market value of nanotechnology products in a range of USD 1 trillion to USD 3.1 trillion by 2015 (see Table 1.3).

The most optimistic forecasts are based on the total market value of all end products in any way connected with nanotechnology, rather than the proportion of end products directly attributable to the value added by nanotechnology. They are therefore rather inflated. It is also important to stress that these forecasts do not integrate the effects of the recent economic crisis, which may prove to have hit science-based technologies hard owing to their need for risk-tolerant, long-term investments. Real or perceived concerns about EHS and ELS issues are also not taken into account.

Table 1.3. Selection of global market forecasts for nanotech-enabled products

USD billions

	2005	2006	2007	2008	2009	2010	2011	2012	2013	2014	2015
LuxResearch (2006, 2008)	30		147							2600	3100
BCC (2008)			12	13			27				
Cientifica (2008)				167				263			1500
RNCOS (2006)						1000					
Wintergreen (2004)											750
Evolution Capital (2001)	105					700					
NSF (2001)	54										1000

Source: Publicly available information on private market forecasts.

The creation of new companies, or the diversification of established ones towards businesses that incorporate nanotechnology, will eventually affect the labour market. One approach to assessing the labour market impact is to extrapolate the number of workers required in the future from the current users of key instrumentation (*e.g.* AFMs and STMs). The National Science Foundation (NSF) applied this approach in 2001 to predict a demand for as many as 2 million new nanotechnology workers worldwide by 2015, of which 0.8-0.9 million in the United States, 0.5-0.6 million in Japan, 0.3-0.4 million in Europe, about 0.2 million in the Asia-Pacific region and 0.1 million in other regions (Roco and Bainbridge, 2001). Most of these jobs were predicted in small and medium-sized companies.

Others have analysed nanotechnology job announcements and skill requirements. For example, Stephan *et al.* (2007) found that the number of such announcements grew from 2002 to 2005, but from a very low starting level. Singh (2007) analysed the demand for nanotechnology skills in Europe and concluded that there is demand for specialised skills in certain areas and for generalists who can operate instruments and nanoscale manufacturing tools. Beyond these studies there is little evidence on the number of jobs created by nanotechnology. The economic crisis adds further uncertainty to the impact of nanotechnology on the labour market.

Objectives and structure of the report

This is the final report of the OECD Working Party on Nanotechnology (WPN) project on nanotechnology impacts on companies and business environments. Its objective has been to contribute to the understanding of nanotechnology and its impacts on companies and business environments through a broad, internationally comparable analysis based on qualitative insights. Specifically, it has sought to learn whether nanotechnology introduces new and specific challenges for companies which may require specific policy responses. The project has involved compiling available indicators and statistics, reviewing previous studies, and undertaking 51 company case studies across 17 countries, covering various nanotechnology sub-areas and fields of application.

The report is structured as follows. Chapter 2 reviews earlier studies on the sources of innovation in nanotechnology, its impacts on company activities, and facilitating factors and barriers in the business environment, application and commercialisation of nanotechnology. It provides a basis for interpreting how the case studies add to previous knowledge. In Chapter 3 attention shifts to the case studies undertaken by the countries participating in the WPN. It presents the case study methodology and the characteristics of the companies interviewed, before turning to the findings and their interpretation. The discussion is structured according to the main themes addressed by the case study questionnaire. Chapter 4 reviews the case studies findings in the light of previous studies, raises policy issues and discusses their implications.

References

BCC Research (2008), *Nanotechnology: A Realistic Market Assessment.*

Cientifica (2008), *The Nanotechnology Opportunity Report.* 3rd edition.

Dandolopartners (2006), Nanotechnology business survey.

Evolution Capital (2001), *Nanotechnology: Commercial Opportunity,* London, Evolution Capital

Hall, Storrs (2005), Nanofuture. Promenthus Books.

Heinze, T. (2004), "Nanoscience and Nanotechnology in Europe: Analysis of Publications and Patent Applications including Comparisons with the United States", *Nanotechnology, Law & Business*, vol. 1.4.

Helpman, E. (ed.) (1998), *General Purpose Technologies and Economic Growth*, MIT Press.

Huang, Z., H. Chan, Z.-K. Chen and M. Rocco (2004), "International Nanotechnology Development in 2003. Country, institution, and technology field analysis based on USPTO patent database", *Journal of Nanoparticle Research* 6.

Hullmann, A. (2007), "Measuring and Assessing the Development of Nanotechnology", *Scientometrics*, vol. 70, no.3 (see also "The Economic Development of Nanotechnology – An indicators-based analysis", European Commission, DG Research, and "Who is Winning the Global Nanorace?". *Nature* (2006), vol. 1.

Kaiser, D. (2006), "Notes toward a Nanotech Timeline", OSTI Working Paper 6-06-001, Office of Science and Technical Information.

Li, X., T. Lin, H. Chen and M. Roco (2007), "Worldwide Nanotechnology Development: A Comparative Study of USPTO, EPO and JPO Patents (1976-2004)", *Journal of Nanoparticle Research* 9.

Lipsey, R., K. Carlaw and C. Bekar (2005), *Economic Transformations – General Purpose Technologies and Long-Term Economic Growth.* Oxford University Press.

LuxResearch (2006), *The Nanotech Report*, 4th edition.

LuxResearch (2008), "Overhyped technology starts to reach potential: nanotech to impact $3.1 trillion in manufactured goods in 2015".

Malanowski, N., T. Heimar, W. Luther, and M. Werner (2006), "Growth Market Nanotechnology – An Analysis of Technology and Innovation", Wiley VCH Verlag.

McNiven, C. (2007), "Overview and Discussion of the Results of the Pilot Survey on Nanotechnology in Canada", Statistics Canada, Working Paper, BBF0006XIE, no. 005.

NCMS and NSF (2006), 2005 NCMS Survey of Nanotechnology in the US Manufacturing Industry.

Noyons, E., R. Buter, A. van Raan, U. Schmooch, T. Heinze, S. Hinze, and R. Rangnow (2003), Mapping Excellence in Science and Technology across Europe Nanoscience and Nanotechnology, final report to the European Commission.

NSF (2001), Societal Implications of Nanoscience and Nanotechnologies. Arlington Virginia, National Science Foundation.

OECD (2005), "Opportunities and Risks of Nanotechnologies", report in co-operation with the OECD International Futures Programme, OECD and Allianz.

OECD (2007), "Capturing Nanotechnology's State of Development via Analysis of Patents", STI Working Paper 2007/4, Directorate for Science, Technology and Industry, *www.oecd.org/sti/working-papers*.

OECD (2009), Nanotechnology: An Overview based on Indicators and Statistics, STI Working Paper 2009/7, Directorate for Science, Technology and Industry, *www.oecd.org/sti/working-papers*.

Perez, C. (2002), *Technological Revolutions and Financial Capital: The Dynamics of Bubbles and Golden Ages*, Edward Elgar.

RNCOS (2006), *The World Nanotechnology Market*.

Roco, M. and W. Bainbridge (eds.) (2001), "Converging Technologies for Improving Human Performance", NSF Report, Arlington, VA.

Roco, M. (2007), "The NNI: Past, Present and Future", in W.A. Goddard *et al.*, *Handbook on Nanoscience, Engineering and Technology*, CRC, Taylor and Francis, Boca Raton and London.

Scheu, M., V. Veefkind, Y. Verbrandt, E. Molina, R. Galan, A. Absalom, and W. Forster (2006), "Mapping Nanotechnology Patents: The EPO Approach", *World Patent Information* 28.

Singh, K.A. (2007), "Nanotechnology Skills and Survey – Summary of Outcomes". Nanoforum report.

Stephan, P., G. Black and T. Chang (2007), The Small Size of the Small Scale Market: The Early-stage Labor Market for Highly Skilled Nanotechnology Workers, *Research Policy* 36, 887-892.

True Nano (year unknown), published by National Institute of Science and Technology Policy, MEXT.

Wintergreen (2004), Nanotechnology Market Opportunities, Market Forecasts and Market Strategies 2004-2009, Wintergreen Research.

Zucker, L. and M. Darby (2005), Socio-economic Impact of Nanoscale Science: Initial Results and Nanobank. NBER Working Paper 11181.

Chapter 2

Insights from previous studies on nanotechnology developments and commercialisation

This chapter reviews a selection of previous studies on nanotechnology developments and commercialisation as a backdrop for the company case studies. Publication and patent data highlight the interdisciplinary, science-based and market-driven, nature of nanotechnology. However, case studies and surveys also point to challenges that companies face, ranging from bottlenecks in funding, human resources and process scalability of R&D. Some of these challenges may be more severe for smaller companies that seek to enter established value chains, while larger companies can benefit from critical mass and complementary assets in R&D and related instrumentation. IPR issues and public perception of nanotechnology can also complicate the business environment.

Key issues addressed in previous studies

For a long time mainstream economics paid little attention to the role of innovation and entrepreneurship in economic growth and development. Since the 1980s, however, theoretical work has started to incorporate technological change as an important endogenous, internally generated factor for productivity and economic growth (see Fagerberg, 2005, for an overview). There has also been increasing interest in understanding emerging technologies and innovation of a more discontinuous nature. This interest mainly stems from studies on information and communication technology (ICT), biotechnology and now nanotechnology, all of which are considered to offer a springboard for a wide range of applications and thus contribute to long-term productivity increases and economic growth.

While the emergence and implications of ICT and biotechnology have been extensively studied, far less is known about nanotechnology. Previous studies on nanotechnology have largely addressed traditional issues in the economics of technological change. These issues are the *sources of nanotechnology-related innovation* (hereafter referred to as nanotechnology innovation), the *impact of nanotechnology on company activities,* and *facilitating factors and barriers in the business environment.* Studies on the sources of nanotechnology innovation have considered the nature of underlying scientific developments, technology transfer between university and industry, and the role of supporting institutions and clusters. Studies on the impacts of nanotechnology on companies have assessed the degree to which it represents a discontinuous technology and may therefore require new technical and managerial skills, as well as its consequences for commercialisation. Finally, studies on facilitating factors and barriers in the nanotechnology business environment have focused on intellectual property rights (IPRs) and public perception of some environmental, health and safety (EHS) risks.

The following discussion reviews previous studies in so far as they address themes that were addressed by the case studies. Preference is given to studies published in peer-reviewed scientific journals (see Meyer, 2007, and OECD, 2008, for lengthier literature reviews).

Sources of nanotechnology innovation

Science and technology transfer

In the absence of other data, publications and patents have primarily been used to consider the sources of innovation and the nature of the scientific knowledge based on nanotechnology. As mentioned, nanotechnology publications appeared earlier and increased more rapidly than patenting and tend to draw on existing fields of science, notably physics, biology and chemistry (Rafols and Meyer, 2007; Rafols, 2007; Zucker *et al.*, 2007). Analyses of patenting suggest cross-pollination, or convergence, particularly between nanotechnology and biotechnology (Grodal and Thoma, 2007). These studies lend further support to a view of nanotechnology as broad-based and convergent by nature (*e.g.* NBIC).

In addition, analyses of publications and patents point to the strength of the linkages between nanotechnology and the sciences. This is commonly noticed by examining patent citations to scientific publications. The higher the share of such citations, the more the patents are considered science-based. When applied to nanotechnology, this type of analysis clearly shows that nanotechnology patents to a greater extent than other technologies draw on scientific publications rather than other patents (OECD, 2009; also Meyer, 2006; Igami and Okazaki, 2007).

Box 2.1. A taxonomy of sectoral patterns of innovation

Various taxonomies classify industries by their sources of innovation. Pavitt (1984) introduced a very influential taxonomy of the sources of innovation in industry (see *e.g.* Marsili, Orietta, 2003, for refinements of this taxonomy):

1. Scale-intensive sectors are characterised by innovation activities for which learning by doing plays a major role. Typically, scale-intensive sectors are populated by large companies producing consumer durables.

2. In supplier-dominated sectors smaller and specialised supplier companies play a main role for innovation; these companies interact and learn through collaboration with larger companies. Examples include stone, glass or other material-producing sectors.

3. Specialised supplier sectors mainly consist of small and science-based companies producing highly specialised components and machinery for other companies. Primary examples are engineering, electronics and instruments.

4. Science-based sectors are characterised by innovation activities that draw on institutionalised R&D (universities, corporate laboratories), close interaction between science and technology during innovation, and technology transfer from universities to industry. Large companies play a major role, as exemplified by the pharmaceuticals and microelectronics sectors.

Source: Pavitt (1984).

Although nanotechnology does not possess the characteristics of an industrial sector, its sources of innovation bear some resemblance to "science-based sectors". Science-based sectors (pharmaceuticals is probably the best example) are characterised by the concentration of R&D in university and corporate labs of larger corporations and by scientific developments and technology transfer from academia to industry. In the case of nanotechnology, universities also play a relatively more important role in patenting when compared with the general situation. Further, in industry, R&D and patenting appear to be concentrated in the corporate laboratories of larger companies (OECD, 2008). However, far less is known about opportunities and bottlenecks for transferring nanotechnology from universities to industry.

One of the first studies on technology transfer in nanotechnology focused on the sources of academic entrepreneurship in the United States (Darby and Zucker, 2003). It concluded that such entrepreneurship is more likely when "star scientists" are involved. These are defined as scientists with many high-impact publications. It is suggested that their importance is due to the tacit knowledge they possess for using complex instrumentation (Bonaccorsi and Thoma, 2007, draw a similar conclusion from European evidence). Other studies suggest that entrepreneurial activity in nanotechnology tends to cluster in regions with experience in related sciences, with top-level universities or research institutes, or with R&D laboratories of major companies (Martin-Fernandez and Leevers, 2004; Robinson *et al.,* 2007; Youtie and Shapira, 2008).

A study by Palmberg (2008) looks at challenges for transferring nanotechnology from universities to industry (Figure 2.1) in Finland. University researchers view their basic research orientation as the most significant challenge. Researchers in industry highlight the identification of commercial opportunities in university research, university researchers' lack of business skills, and underdeveloped manufacturing technologies as the core challenges. Further, university researchers' basic research orientation appears to be an inhibiting factor for patenting and licensing of nanotechnology research.

The different perceptions of university researchers and company inventors, at least in the Finnish case, may be due to the interdisciplinary and science-based nature of nanotechnology. For example, theoretical physicists play an important role in nanotechnology but may be unaccustomed to collaborating with companies, especially in traditional industries in which other branches of science (such as chemistry or biology) play an important role. Interdisciplinary collaboration may also require specific organisational and institutional arrangements. These may be especially important in nano-technology although Llerena and Meyer-Krahmer (2003) have identified similar types of interdisciplinarity in other fields.

Figure 2.1 Challenges for technology transfer: university researchers versus companies

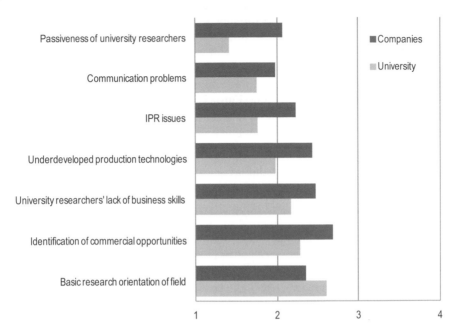

Note: All differences statistically significant at 5% level. The results are based on 476 survey responses. The x-axis measures the degree of importance of challenges on a scale from 1-4.

Source: Palmberg (2008).

Applications and drivers of demand

While the characteristics of nanotechnology innovation resemble those generally observed in science-based sectors, many applications are more directly driven by market demand and customer needs. In this respect nanotechnology may differ from biotechnology but resemble ICT. Biotechnology, especially in its application in pharmaceuticals, is considered a prime example of a science-based sector. In ICT, scientific developments have been important but the main sources of innovation relates to markets, the development of services and standardisation, not least in the field of mobile telecommunications where standards have created sophisticated demand for technologies and huge markets. Overall, nanotechnology may thus be characterised as a science-based but market-driven field, even though the science aspects may currently be in the foreground.

The role of market demand and customer needs as a driver for nanotechnology innovation is best discussed in the context of "top-down" and "bottom-up" approaches to nanoscale engineering. The top-down approach is currently more clearly driven by market demand. As discussed above, this may primarily concern applications in the electronics industry, as nanotechnology can offer a new means of maintaining capacity increases in microprocessors (and uphold "Moore's Law") and help the industry to respond to demand for increasingly capacity-hungry products and systems. These possibilities create a powerful incentive for R&D and innovation in this industry; they are also frequently highlighted in recent industry-commissioned roadmaps and other foresight exercises.

Other nanotechnology applications may also be largely demand-driven. For example, a recent market forecast from 2008 highlights the materials and manufacturing sectors, including many traditional industries such as textiles, as likely to be most affected by nanotechnology (Cientifica, 2008). It is argued that demand for new functionalities of existing materials is more clearly specified in these sectors than in high-technology sectors, which are subject to far greater technological and market uncertainties. As discussed earlier, nanotechnology can also help to address broader socio-economic concerns such as energy shortages, accessible health care, clean water and climate change. All of these give companies demand-based incentives; in some cases demand-led innovation policies (*e.g.* standardisation and public technology procurement) may play an important role in creating new markets for nanotechnology.

Impact of nanotechnology on company activities

Incremental versus discontinuous technology

While traditional models of innovation and economic growth have tended to treat technological change in terms of repeated and continuous (incremental) innovation, the more recent literature has taken a greater interest in innovation that embodies more radical, or discontinuous, technologies. These may have a greater impact on companies as they often require new competences and may disrupt the competence base of companies. A recurring theme has been the relative strengths of established companies and start-ups when facing discontinuous technologies, and how companies manage knowledge and other resources in such situations. As nanotechnology is often presented as a radical technology with potentially widespread and profound impacts (a potential general purpose technology) this theme calls for further consideration.

A seminal model of company dynamics has been proposed to trace the role of different types of companies and managerial strategies over the lifecycle of an emerging technology (Abernathy and Utterback, 1978; Adner and Zemsky, 2003; and, more recently, Christensen, 2007). When a discontinuous technology emerges, related innovative opportunities are very uncertain. New companies enter and engage in experimental R&D. Gradually, these experiments converge around the most viable application: a so-called dominant design. Innovation increasingly focuses on a fewer set of applications and the advantages of new companies fade in favour of established ones which can draw on their greater in-house R&D, manufacturing and marketing capabilities. In the maturing phase of the technology lifecycle the locus of competition shifts from innovation to price as the production of variations of a given dominant design commences. New companies may exit or merge with established companies and the industry tends to consolidate (see Rothaermel, 2001, and Hill and Rothaermel, 2003, for recent elaborations of the seminal model).

Shea (2005) highlighted specific features of nanotechnology which pertain to the degree of discontinuity it may introduce. She acknowledges that nanotechnology has characteristics of a general purpose technology and that it is well placed to spread in many industrial sectors, for many different uses, and therefore also to have varying degrees of impact on companies (see Youtie *et al.*, 2008, for recent discussions of nanotechnology as a general purpose technology). Accordingly, nanotechnology may enable both incremental and discontinuous innovation. The top-down approach to nanoscale engineering may represent the incremental aspect and favour established companies, while the bottom-up approach is probably more discontinuous and may therefore favour the entry of new companies (see also Avenel *et al.*, 2007).

Rothaermel and Thursby (2007) suggest that developments in nanotechnology, unlike those in biotechnology, may depend more on physical (*e.g.* instrumentation, machinery) than on human capital. This may favour large and established companies from the start. The argument is that while biotechnology and nanotechnology have similarities in their early science-based phase, the diffusion patterns of key inventions differ in important respects. Recombinant DNA techniques were invented in a university setting, and their widespread industrial use depended on the availability of specialised personnel. As a result, it took almost two decades for the techniques to gain widespread industrial use (through the invention of the automatic DNA sequencer). For nanotechnology the role of instrumentation, such as STM and AFM, has been more important. These instruments were developed for industrial use in the laboratories of large and established companies (IBM), and therefore diffused much more rapidly to a range of industries. This suggests that established companies may be better positioned that new entries to assimilate nanotechnology, in contrast to the situation for biotechnology.

Barriers to commercialisation

Some governments have commissioned company surveys to investigate barriers to the commercialisation of nanotechnology. A comparison of surveys across countries is tricky owing to differences in methodologies, themes covered, and questions included; responses naturally depend on the alternatives respondents are offered for particular questions. These differences should be kept in mind for the following description of some results of survey work in the United States, Australia, Germany and Finland on barriers to commercialisation of nanotechnology.

The US survey was undertaken by the National Center for Manufacturing Sciences (NCMS) in 2003 and 2005 (with a third round in 2009). It covered 595 senior executives of companies listed as subscribers to *Small Times Magazine*. The overall aim of the NCMS survey was to determine whether these executives perceived and treated nanotechnology differently from any other generation of advanced science and technology. The survey proposed 18 key challenges to the respondents, and the rankings are illustrated in Figure 2.2.

The survey identified high processing costs, followed by lengthy times to market, insufficient investment capital, poor process scalability and intellectual property (IP) issues as the main challenges. *High processing costs for nanotechnology products* is taken as an indication that the nanomanufacturing industry is still in its infancy and characterised by few early adopters, fragmented markets, lack of infrastructure equipment for nanoscale manufacturing, and few efficient manufacturing methods. The *lack of investment capital* primarily relates to the high cost of building and maintaining processing facilities. Further, many academic entrepreneurs with a background in natural sciences (physics, chemistry, biology) tend to lack essential business and entrepreneurial skills, and may be unable to explain the value proposition of their products to potential investors or customers. *Lengthy times to market* of nanotechnology products combined with uncertainties over public perceptions of EHS issues can compound the difficulties.

In this survey *poor process scalability* is also considered as a challenge that is specific to nanotechnology, *e.g.* challenges in the transition from R&D to pilot and industrial scale production. The poor process scalability of nanotechnology processes and the integration of nanoparticles into dissimilar materials with reproducible performance and properties are highlighted as challenges, especially in converging nanotechnology and biotechnology areas. Breakthroughs would be needed to make the transition from lab-scale to pilot and prototype manufacturing. Finally, *EHS concerns* span several key areas, such as the handling and industrial use of nanoparticles, coatings, nanoadditives and nanotubes. The key challenges include the development and demonstration of targeted applications for societal benefits and addressing the safety and regulatory issues associated with such products.

Figure 2.2. Challenges in nanotechnology-related manufacturing and commercialisation amongst US companies

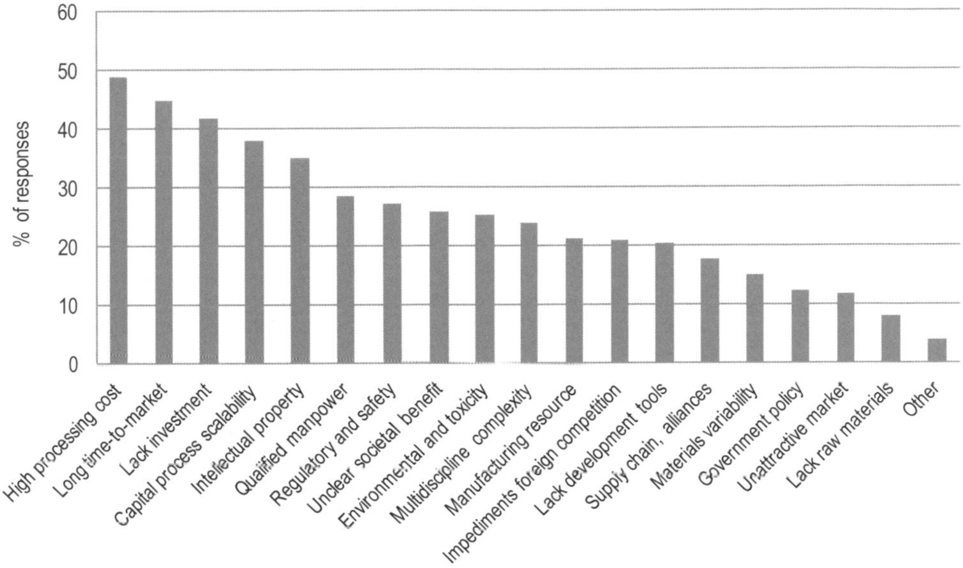

Source: NCMS and NSF (2006).

Malanowski *et al.* (2006) present the results of a German survey carried out in 2006, which obtained responses from 107 companies, a majority of which were smaller start-ups. A question was asked about the "obstacles to successful nanotechnology applications in 2006" across nine different response alternatives ranging from costs and funding, lack of skilled personnel, partners, information, market potential and legislation. Of these items the lack of financial resources, funding and other financial support tops the list of barriers, while the lack of necessary information to pursue the applications, a lack of market potential and legislative issues are at the bottom. As financial issues generally rank high in surveys on innovation (see Parvan, 2007, for results of a recent EU Community Innovation Survey), it is not clear whether there is anything specific to nanotechnology in this ranking.

A survey undertaken by Dandolopartners for the Australian government in 2006 targeted 134 companies with a documented interest in nanotechnology based on a random sample of a longer list of companies (Dandolopartners, 2006). This survey framed the issue of barriers in terms of a question on various elements that prevented the companies from investing in nanotechnology. The lack of customer demand for nanotechnology products was given as the major barrier, followed by difficulties in acquiring the right skills in house to manage the development process. Less significant issues were the lack of access to prototype or testing facilities for nanotechnology products and the lack of access to information about relevant research.

In Finland Spinverse (see *www.tekes.fi/eng/* and the FinNano programme home page) has also undertaken company surveys. The first survey in 2004 covered 61 companies and the latest in 2006 covered 134. In this case the question was posed as follows: "What have you found to be the main challenges when commercialising nanotechnology?" Answer items ranged from the identification of commercial applications during collaboration with universities, lack of standards or customer/consumer acceptance, to difficulties in achieving reliable mass production and shortage of funding. The major barriers were identified as difficulties in achieving reliable mass production, shortage of funding and challenges in identifying commercial applications; lack of standards was considered less relevant.

Impacts on value chains

Barriers to commercialisation vary with companies' position in value chains. LuxResearch, a consultancy, should be credited with sketching a nanotechnology value chain, a model that has since been much referred to (LuxResearch, 2006). The first upstream segment of this value chain comprises producers of raw materials (*e.g.* carbon nanotubes, quantum dots, fullerenes). The next segment is populated by companies using nanotechnology raw materials to develop intermediate products with nanoscale features, such as coatings, composite materials, memory and logic chips, orthopaedic material, etc. Many companies in this segment are start-ups. The third segment, further downstream, is mainly populated by larger companies that develop nano-enabled end products based on the intermediate products. The instrumentation companies are highlighted as a fourth element.

Maine and Garnsey (2006) have undertaken empirical work on nanotechnology value chains based on company interviews. They focus on commercialisation challenges of new ventures (company start-ups) in the upstream segments of the nanotechnology value chain, highlighting the challenges these ventures face for managing scientific and technological developments, on the one hand, and market needs, on the other. According to the study, the science-based nature of nanotechnology, and its broad applicability, implies that replication of laboratory attributes in prototypes and production processes is very complex, demanding and expensive. As nanomaterials are often used in larger product systems (for example nano-coatings for car engines) interoperability between materials, components and the whole system is also important. These issues introduce high levels of technological and market uncertainties for commercialisation.

Facilitating factors and barriers in business environment

IPR issues

Appropriation of innovation refers to the abilities of companies to protect their innovations through intellectual property rights (IPRs) and thereby secure commercial returns on their R&D and other investments. The literature on factors that facilitate and inhibit the appropriation of innovation is substantial. It makes clear that companies can protect their IPRs in many ways, ranging from secrecy, achieving lead times and other first mover advantages, preferential supplier contacts, product complexity, etc. (see Levin *et al.*, 1987), but patenting has received the most attention. This is also the case for nanotechnology and there is now a burgeoning literature on the nature and strategies of patenting in this field.

The common thread in most studies has been the specificities of nanotechnology and the implications for practices at patent offices and for companies' intellectual property (IP) management strategies. On patent offices, Bleeker and Uhlir (2007) suggest that the emerging nature of nanotechnology makes it difficult to identify the prior art in order to determine whether patent applications should be granted. This is especially the case when new keywords appear in the patent applications, such as those relating to new types of nanomaterials. Patent examiners need specialised technical knowledge in multiple fields to avoid issuing overly broad (and possibly unenforceable) patent claims. Miller and Harris (2006) support this through a case study on patenting in the area of carbon nanotubes. Carbon nanotubes display extraordinary electrical, mechanical, chemical and thermal properties and might therefore be used as a platform technology in a very wide range of industries. Miller and Harris believe that the commercial promise of carbon nanotubes has resulted in a frenzy of patenting and overly broad patent claims, and created a dense thicket of interlocking and over-lapping patents.

The overall impression is that patent thickets can mount a significant barrier both for company entry and for nanotechnology innovation more generally. The costs of navigating patent thickets may be high and can outweigh some of the commercial gains, especially for smaller companies that may be less familiar with patenting practices and IP management issues. While companies in other fields – mobile telecommunications is a prime example – are employing advanced strategies and have relevant institutional mechanisms in place, the situation for nanotechnology appears much more uncertain. Questions have also been raised about the effect of ongoing patent regulatory reform on nanotechnology patenting and whether completely new institutional arrangements would be needed (Axford, 2006; Miller and Harris, 2006; Maebius, 2007; also Hullmann and Frycêk, 2007).

Public perceptions and EHS issues

History suggests that public perceptions of emerging technologies can have long-lasting effects on their possibilities for generating innovation, diffusing and being used throughout industries and society. ICT and biotechnology again offer some perspective. Freeman (2003) considers why in his view biotechnology may not emerge as a general purpose technology of the 21st century while ICT is doing so. Among other things, he links the slow industrial uptake and societal use of some biotechnology with problems of social and political acceptance. In contrast, ICT has been extremely widely accepted, as the popularity of such terms as "information society" and "knowledge economy" demonstrates.

There are still only a few empirical studies on public perceptions of nanotechnology. Amongst them are four extensive and comparable studies: one by the Nanotechnology Research Institute of AIST in Japan; one by Cobb and Macoubrie (2004) in the United States; one by the Royal Society and the Royal Academy of Engineering (2004) in the United Kingdom; and one carried out by the Department of Industry, Tourism and Resources in Australia (2007). All of these studies target the public at large and thus analyse representative samples, although certain country-specific issues may affect the results (see Table 2.1).

Fujita (2006) reports on a study covering 1 011 individuals in the greater Tokyo area of Japan, which also included assessments of other technology areas such as solar energy, IT and the Internet, biotechnology/genetic engineering, nuclear technology, and mobile phones. Of these technology areas most respondents perceived solar energy as contributing to quality of life (80% of the respondents), followed by information technology (IT) and the Internet (60%), biotechnology/genetic engineering (55%), and nano-technology (50%). Among these, 55% claimed to have heard relatively frequently about nanotechnology and considered health care and environ-mental applications especially beneficial.

Very similar results emerge from the Australian study, summarised by the Department of Industry, Tourism and Resources (2007). Out of a sample of 1 000 persons, 63% claimed to have heard of the term nanotechnology even though a majority of these reported limited understanding of the field. The Australian study only covered nanotechnology and reports an even higher percentage of individuals (83%) who are "hopeful" and "excited" by its potential. The share of people who consider that the benefits outweigh the risks was however only 54%. As in Japan, health care and environmental issues are indicated as the most beneficial areas of application. The main areas of concern were poor surveillance of nanotechnology generally and risks of unethical applications.

Table 2.1. Comparisons of public perceptions of nanotechnology in Japan, Australia, the United Kingdom and the United States

Country	Public awareness of nanotech	Hopeful of nanotech benefits
Japan	55%	88%
Australia	63%	83%
United Kingdom	29%	68%
United States	48%	70%

Source: Fujita (2006); Dept. of Industry, Tourism and Resources (2007).

The United Kingdom and the United States studies are in line with those in Japan and Australia as regards the perceived benefits from nanotechnology. Health care and environmental benefits again scored highest; most fears related to privacy issues, the arms race, and the safety of nanomaterials. Nonetheless, the share of people who are hopeful about the benefits of nanotechnology were lower in both the United Kingdom (68%) and the United States (70%). Public awareness of nanotechnology was also lower in both of these countries (see Table 2.1). The UK study drew on a sample of 1 005 individuals; the US study sample was 1 536.

Summary

The findings from previous studies on nanotechnology developments and commercialisation referred to in this chapter can be summarised in the following points:

- Nanotechnology publications draw on an interdisciplinary knowledge base (physics, chemistry and biology), and patent data highlight interactions between nanotechnology and biotechnology and the science-based nature of developments. However, there are also fields of application in which market demand is the main driver.

- Nanotechnology, unlike biotechnology, may depend more on physical (instrumentation, machinery, etc.) than on human capital. This may favour larger established companies more than start-ups as they possess critical mass in terms of financial resources, R&D laboratories and complementary assets (*e.g.* complementary technologies).

- Company surveys highlight barriers to commercialisation. These mainly relate to the complexity of nanotechnology R&D and its poor process scalability, bottlenecks in human resources, and funding. The typical position of start-up companies in upstream segments of value chains can increase technical and market uncertainties for these companies.

- The interdisciplinary and enabling nature of nanotechnology may lead to overly broad patent claims which create thickets of interlocking and overlapping patents. Patent thickets may create barriers to entry for companies and can lead to additional challenges for IP management.

- Public perceptions of nanotechnology seem to be currently quite positive, especially in terms of health care and environmental applications. However, awareness of nanotechnology differs across countries.

References

Abernathy, W and J. Utterback (1978), "Patterns of Innovation in Industry", *Technology Review*, vol. 80, no. 7, June-July.

Adner, R and P. Zemsky (2003), "A Demand-based Perspective on Sustainable Competitive Advantage", *Strategic Management Journal*, 27.

Avenel, E, V. Mangematin, and C. Rieu (2007), "Diversification and Hybridization in Firm Knowledge Bases in Nanotechnology", *Research Policy* 36, 6.

Axford, L.A. (2006), "Patent Drafting Considerations for Nanotechnology Inventions", *Nanotechnology Law & Business*, vol. 3, no. 3.

Bleeker, R and N. Uhlir (2007), "A Small Charge of Infringement: Strategic Alternatives for Nanotech Patent Defenders", *Nanotechnology Law & Business*, vol. 4, no. 4.

Bonaccorsi, A and G. Thoma (2007), "Institutional Complementarity and Inventive Performance in Nano Science and Technology", *Research Policy*, vol. 36, Issue 6.

Christensen, C. (2007), *The Innovator's Dilemma*, Harvard Business School Press.

Cientifica (2008), "Nanotechnologies in 2009. Creative Destruction or Credit Crunch?", White Paper.

Cobb, M. and J. Macourbrie (2004), "Public Perceptions about Nanotechnology: Risks, Benefits and Trust", *Journal of Nanoparticle Research* 6.

Dandolopartners (2006), "Nanotechnology Business Survey. A report for Department of Industry, Tourism and Resources", Australian Government and Nanotechnology Victoria, Ltd.

Darby, M. and M. Zucker (2003), "Grilichesian Breakthroughs: Inventions of Methods of Inventing and Firm Entry in Nanotechnology", NBER Working Paper 9825.

Department of Industry, Tourism and Resources, Australia (2007), Final report: Australian community attitudes held about nanotechnology – Trends 2005 to 2007, Market Attitude Research Services.

Fagerberg, J. (2005), "Innovation: A Guide to the Literature", in J. Fagerberg, D. Mowery and R. Nelson (eds.), *The Oxford Handbook of Innovation*, Oxford University Press.

Freeman, C. (2003), "Policies for Developing New Technologies", SPRU Electronic Working Paper Series, no. 98.

Fujita, Y. (2006), "Perception of Nanotechnology among General Public in Japan", *Asia-Pacific Nanotech Weekly*, vol. 4, article no. 2.

Grodal, S. and G. Thoma (2007), "Cross-pollination in Science and Technology: The Emergence of the Nanobio Subfield", unpublished draft.

Hill, C.W.L., F.T. Rothaermel (2003), "The Performance of Incumbent Firms in the Face of Radical Technological Innovation", *Academy of Management Review*, 28 (2).

Hullmann, A and R. Frycek (2007), "IPR in Nanotechnology – Lessons from Experiences Worldwide", proceedings, 2 May.

Igami, M. and T. Okazaki (2007), "Capturing Nanotechnology's Current State of Development via Analysis of Patents", *OECD Science, Technology and Industry Working Papers* 2007/4, Directorate for Science, Technology and Industry, OECD, Paris, *www.oecd.org/sti/working-papers*.

Levin, A., R. Klevorick, S. Nelson, R. Winter, and Z. Griliches (1987), "Appropriating the Returns from Industrial Research and Development", *Brookings Papers on Economic Activity*, no. 3.

Llerena, P. and F. Meyer-Krahmer (2003), "Interdisciplinary Research and the Organisation of University: General Challenges and a Case Study", in A. Geuna, A. Slater and E. Steinmuller (eds.), *Science and Innovation: Rethinking the Rationales for Funding and Governance*, Edward Edgar.

LuxResearch (2006), *The Nanotech Report*, fourth edition.

Maebius, S. (2007), "Patent Reform Bill: Will It Benefit Nanotechnology?" *Nanotechnology Law and Business*, vol. 4, no. 2.

Maine, E. and E. Garnsey (2006), "Commercializing Generic Technology: The Case of Advanced Materials Ventures", *Research Policy* 35.

Malanowski, N., T. Heimar, W. Luther, and M. Werner (2006), "Growth Market Nanotechnology – An Analysis of Technology and Innovation", Wiley VCH Verlag.

Marsili, Orietta (2003), *The Anatomy and Evolution of Industries: Technological Change and Industrial Dynamics*, Edward Elgar, Cheltenham, UK.

Martinez-Fernandez, M.C. and K. Leevers (2004), "Knowledge Creation, Sharing and Transfer as an Innovation Strategy: The Discovery of Nano-technology by South West Sydney", *International Journal of Technology Management*, vol. 28, no. 3-6.

Meyer, M. (2006), "Are Patenting Scientists the Better Scholars?: An Exploratory Comparison of Inventor-Authors with their Non-inventing Peers in Nano-science and Technology", *Research Policy*, vol. 35, no. 10.

Meyer, M. (2007), "What Do We Know about Innovation in Nanotechnology? Some propositions about an emerging field between hype and path-dependency", *Scientometrics*, vol. 70, no. 3.

Miller, J. and D. Harris (2006), "The Carbon Nanotube Patent Landscape", *Nanotechnology Law & Business*, vol. 3, no. 4.

NCMS and NSF (2006), 2005 NCMS Survey of Nanotechnology in the US Manufacturing Industry.

OECD (2008), *Open Innovation and Global Networks*, OECD, Paris.

OECD (2009), "Nanotechnology: An Overview based on Indicators and Statistics, *OECD Science, Technology and Industry Working Papers* 2009/7, Directorate for Science, Technology and Industry, OECD, Paris, *www.oecd.org/sti/working-papers.*

Palmberg, C. (2008), "The Transfer and Commercialisation of Nanotechnology: A Comparative Analysis of University and Company Researchers", *Journal of Technology Transfer*, vol. 33, no. 6.

Parvan, S.V. (2007), "Community Innovation Statistics, Is Europe Growing More Innovative?", *Statistics in Focus, Science and Technology*, 61/2007.

Pavitt, K. (1984), "Sectoral Patterns of Technical Change: Towards a Taxonomy and a Theory", *Research Policy* 13.

Rafols, I. and M. Meyer (2007), "How Cross-disciplinary is Bionanotechnology? Explanations in the speciality of molecular motors", *Scientometrics*, vol. 70, no.3.

Rafols, I. (2007), "Strategies for Knowledge Acquisition in Bionanotechnology: Why are Interdisciplinary Practices Less Widespread than Expected?", *Innovation: the European Journal of Social Science Research*, 20(4).

Robinson, D., A. Rip and V. Mangematin (2007), "Technological Agglomeration and the Emergence of Clusters and Networks in Nanotechnology", *Research Policy* 36.

Rothaermel, F. and M. Thursby (2007), "The Nanotech versus the Biotech Revolution: Sources of Productivity in Incumbent Firm Research", *Research Policy*, vol. 36, no. 6.

Rothaermel, F.T. (2001), "Incumbent's Advantage through Exploiting Complementary Assets via Interfirm Cooperation", *Strategic Management Journal*, 22 (6-7).

Shea, C. (2005), "Future Management Research Directions in Nano-technology: A Case Study", *Journal of Engineering and Technology Management*, vol. 22, no. 3.

The Royal Society & The Royal Academy of Engineering (2004), "Nanoscience and Nanotechnologies: Opportunities and Uncertainties", The Royal Society.

Youtie, J. and P. Shapira (2008), "Emergence of Nanodistricts in the United States", *Economic Development Quarterly*, vol. 22, no. 3, 187-199.

Youtie, J., M. Iacopetta, and S. Graham (2008), Assessing the Nature of Nanotechnology: Can We Uncover an Emerging General Purpose Technology? *Journal of Technology Transfer*, vol. 33, no. 3.

Zucker, L., M. Darby, J. Furner, R. Lio and H. Ma (2007), "Minerva Unbound: Knowledge Stocks, Knowledge Flows and New Technology Production, *Research Policy*, Elsevier, vol. 36(6), pp. 850-863, July.

Chapter 3

Insights from the case studies on the impacts of nanotechnology on companies

This chapter presents the background and findings of the company case studies, including methodological issues and limitations that have to be taken into account. The case study sample is relatively well balanced in terms of nanotechnology sub-areas and fields of application when compared with patenting. Companies highlight the enabling nature of nanotechnology as a main entry driver, even though its share of R&D investments, sales and employment are hard to quantify. The case studies also highlight some variation by company size in the sources of nanotechnology competences and in challenges for commercialisation. The challenges that appear specific to nanotechnology include the complexity of R&D and its poor process scalability, human resource constraints, and concerns about EHS issues. Challenges in the funding of R&D and innovation are also highlighted, although they may be common to start-up companies in science-based technologies in general.

Methodology and limitations of the case studies

This chapter reports the findings of the OECD Working Party on Nanotechnology (WPN) project on "Nanotechnology Impacts on Companies and Business Environments". Broad participation in the project provided an unusual opportunity to undertake internationally comparable company case studies on different nanotechnology sub-areas and fields of application. The development of an appropriate questionnaire required several meetings in May and November 2007, e-mail exchanges and intense collaboration, principally between Canada and Switzerland, the project lead countries, and the OECD Secretariat.

The case study questionnaire was finalised in January 2008. It consisted of four parts. The first part asked for general company information, and the second considered the sources, nature and drivers for a company's involvement in nanotechnology. The third and fourth parts addressed key business challenges and the general impacts of nanotechnology on the company and its industry. The questionnaire also collected some numerical data.

The case studies were planned as face-to-face interviews with company representatives using the questionnaire as a detailed guide for discussion. It was decided only to include companies that have engaged in nanotechnology-related R&D or production although no explicit definition of a nanotechnology company was used. To ensure broad coverage countries were encouraged to select a mixture of start-ups, small and larger companies according to national circumstances. They were also encouraged to address more than one nano-technology sub-area and field of application. Countries were free to approach the selected companies as they judged best. Some sent the questionnaire in advance and followed up with bilateral discussions while others only used face-to-face interviews.

The case studies started in February 2008. The questionnaire was used to design a case study template in order to ensure the inclusion of all insights and key points, as well as contextual information. The aim was to facilitate a concise synthesis of analytically interesting insights to support the analysis of the case studies. Completed questionnaires and templates were requested for every company interviewed.

Owing to delays, the final deadline for completed questionnaires and templates was extended several times. By December 2008, 47 completed questionnaires and templates had been submitted. An additional question-naire and three additional templates were submitted in March 2009. This report is thus based on 51 company case studies from 17 countries. A list of company names is in Annex 3.A, excluding those who wished to remain anonymous. The report has benefitted from discussions on an earlier draft at a project workshop in October 2008 in Helsinki and subsequent comments by delegates and others mentioned in the foreword. Figure 3.1 gives the distribution of the number of company case studies by country.

Figure 3.1. Distribution of company case studies by country

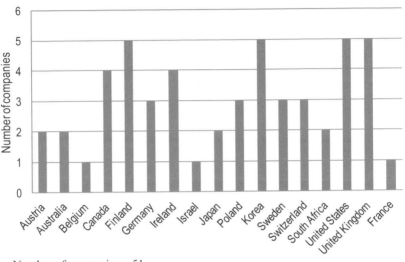

Number of companies = 51.

The main sources for the analysis of the case studies are the numerical information combined with the templates; the latter have also provided company descriptions and citations which are used throughout as examples. The analytical approach loosely draws on the principles of grounded theory to identify, highlight and interpret the case study findings (see Charmaz, 2006, on grounded theory).This methodology identified key issues in the data and groups these under common concepts, or categories, to distil common features across a majority of the cases included in the study. Contrasting insights have been highlighted when deemed interesting although these anecdotal observations may not be representative. This methodological approach provides a basis for relatively robust conclusions about the nature and drivers of companies' involvement in nanotechnology, the key challenges for commercialisation, and impacts on industries and business environments.

A few words on the limitations of the case studies are warranted. A common criticism of case studies is that, unlike statistical analysis, they do not allow for generalisation across a larger population. Case studies should instead be seen as means of identifying and generating a deeper unders-tanding of key issues that relate to a larger population (Yin, 2008). Hence, while the case study sample referred to in this chapter does not represent the whole population of companies involved in nanotechnology, it provides a basis for identifying and gaining a deeper understanding of some key issues. Reference to indicators, statistics and previous studies are intended to help ensure that the case studies identify and analyse key issues, in order to add to previous knowledge.

As already noted, nanotechnology is a multifaceted field with many sub-areas which feed into a broad range of fields of application. Ideally, one would wish to identify and understand key issues in the specific sub-areas and fields of application. The following analysis attempts, in so as far as possible, to do so. However, although the case study sample is relatively large, so detailed an analysis of the findings would reduce the number of observations to the extent that reliable interpretations would be hard to make. It should therefore be stressed that this report falls short of providing a detailed analysis of specific sub-areas and fields of application.[1] Further case studies of specific sub-areas and fields of application would be a logical and valuable continuation of the work carried out for this report.

Company characteristics

The first part of the case study questionnaire requested general information, including the year of establishment, industry, total employees and sales. The second part asked for a description of the nanotechnology area the company is involved in. This information provides a basis for evaluating the characteristics and coverage of the company sample. A strict assessment of the degree to which the company sample is representative of the global population of nanotechnology-related companies is impossible owing to definitional issues and the lack of reliable company registers. Nonetheless, some indication can be gained from comparing the sample with patenting as an indicator for R&D and innovation activity.

Company size distribution

Companies were assigned to size classes by number of employees. The small size cohort refers to companies with 1-49 employees, the medium one to companies with 50-249 employees, and the large one to companies with more than 250 employees.[2] The size distribution of the case study company sample is displayed in Figure 3.2.

Figure 3.2. Company size distribution

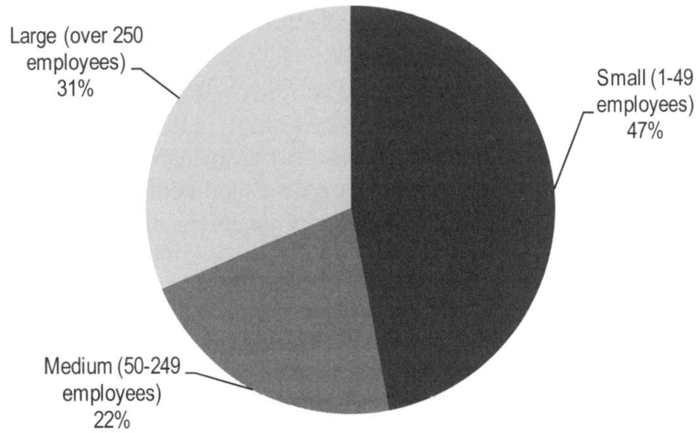

Number of companies = 50.

Small companies take the lead, followed by large and medium-sized companies. Company size may be an important analytical dimension in so far as small and larger companies differ in terms of the nature of, and drivers for, their involvement in nanotechnology and the challenges they face for commercialisation. As discussed in Chapter 2, generalised models of company dynamics suggest that small new companies may, at least initially, be at an advantage for assimilating emerging technologies owing to their flexibility and entrepreneurial nature. As nanotechnology is still in an early phase of development, this may partly explain the predominance of smaller companies in the sample. It may also simply be that they are easier to identify. In larger companies it is harder to assess the role of nano-technology, which is typically only one technology field amongst several that the company draws on.

Nanotechnology sub-areas and fields of application

The case study companies identify many potential applications in different industries. Because of the emerging nature of nanotechnology, companies' activities mainly focus on R&D. For these reasons it is difficult to classify companies by nanotechnology application industries. It makes more sense to classify them by nanotechnology sub-areas and broader technology fields on the basis of on their responses to the questionnaire. Patent classification schemes are used for this purpose as they enable comparisons with nanotechnology patenting. The first scheme breaks nano-technology down into sub-areas and the second aggregates patent technology classes into broader technology fields (see Figure 3.3. for the sub-areas and

Schmoch (2008) for details when aggregating patent classes into broader technology fields). Many of the case study companies are classified in multiple sub-areas and fields of application owing to the broad-based nature of nanotechnology and its applications.

Figure 3.3 shows the distribution of companies by nanotechnology sub-areas along with the share of all nanotechnology patents in these same sub-areas. The majority of companies are active in the areas of nanomaterials, nanoelectronics, instruments and measurement, and nanobiotechnology; there are fewer in nano-optics and none in nanomagnetics. In terms of patenting, nanomaterials and nanoelectronics have been most active; the number of patents is significantly lower in the other sub-areas. Accordingly, it appears that the case study sample represents innovation activities in the field relatively well, although instruments and measurement appears somewhat over-represented.

Figure 3.3. Companies by nanotechnology sub-area

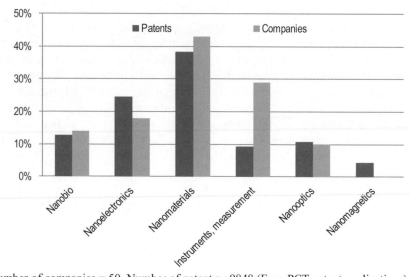

Number of companies = 50. Number of patent s= 9848 (Euro-PCT patent applications).

Figure 3.4. Companies by application field

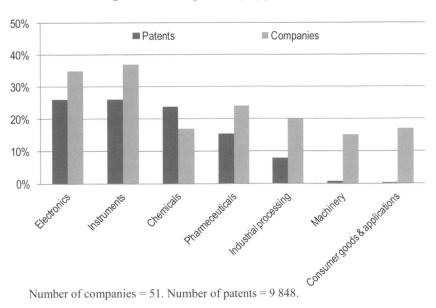

Number of companies = 51. Number of patents = 9 848.

Figure 3.4 shows the distribution of companies by the field of application of their nanotechnology activities. The most common applications are in electronics and instruments, followed by pharmaceuticals and industrial processing. This distribution is roughly in line with patenting trends although industrial processing and machinery appear over-represented in the case study sample. There is less patenting in industrial processing since patenting is less relevant for protection of intellectual property rights (IPRs) in process-intensive industries. The sample also contains a relatively large share of companies in consumer goods applications when compared with patenting.

In the following section, company size and nanotechnology sub-area will be used as analytical dimensions, where possible, to deepen the analysis. Company size takes into account the different role that small and larger companies may play as carriers of technology and innovation in emerging technologies. Sub-areas can provide a somewhat more detailed view of commercialisation and related activities.

As already mentioned, one limitation of using nanotechnology sub-areas as an analytical dimension for this sample is the reduced number of observations. Table 3.1 shows a higher concentration of small companies in nanobiotechnology and a majority of medium-sized companies in instruments. As a consequence, findings related to nanobiotechnology may mainly be relevant for small companies while those related to instruments may apply particularly to medium-sized companies. The sub-areas of nanoelectronics, nanomaterials and nano-optics are more equally distributed among companies of different sizes.

Table 3.1. Distribution of companies by size and nanotechnology sub-area

	Nano-bio	Nano-electronics	Nano-materials	Instruments, measurement	Nano-optics
Small companies	25%	20%	24%	10%	8%
Medium companies	9%	18%	27%	82%	0%
Large companies	6%	31%	50%	6%	6%

It should again be recalled that many of these companies are involved in multiple sub-areas. For this reason, percentages across sub-areas do not add up in Table 3.1 and some of the subsequent figures. The use of multiple classifications is necessary, especially for small companies, as it reflects the experimental nature of their R&D and commercialisation activities. Large companies appear more focused on specific nanotechnology sub-areas, and in particular on those which are more mature (nanoelectronics and nanomaterials) and have progressed further in the commercialisation of nanotechnology (see below).

Nanotechnology entry, activities and drivers

The second part of the case study questionnaire asked for the nature of, and drivers for, companies' involvement and activities in nanotechnology based on the definition provided in Box 3.1. This part of the questionnaire gives further insight into both the nature of nanotechnology developments and the role of nanotechnology in companies' innovation activities.

> **Box 3.1. A definition of nanotechnology (the ISO scoping and WPN working definition as of November 2007)**
>
> Understanding and control of matter and processes at the nanoscale, typically, but not exclusively, below 100 nanometres in one or more dimensions, where the onset of size-dependent phenomena usually enables novel applications. Utilising the properties of nanoscale materials that differ from the properties of individual atoms, molecules, and bulk matter to create improved materials, devices and systems that exploit these new properties.

Entry and drivers

On average the companies had been involved in nanotechnology for 10 years. The average was seven years for smaller and medium-sized companies and 16 years for larger companies. For nanobiotechnology and nanomaterials the average was slightly higher compared with the other sub-areas. When compared with the timeline for nanotechnology developments, the overall average is in line with available data on the acceleration of R&D investments and patenting since the late 1990s. For new nanotechnology-dedicated companies, the number of years since entry naturally coincides with the number of years since their establishment. Some of the larger and more established companies report significantly more variability; some of the large companies had been involved in nanotechnology for from 18 to 33 years.

As Box 3.2 shows, nanotechnology enables companies to enhance existing products through the addition of new functionalities, characteristics or performance attributes (*e.g.* electromagnetic properties, endurance of materials, cost and performance improvements, better energy efficiency) or to develop completely new products that may replace existing ones or open new markets. Usually this involves the introduction of new manufacturing techniques that harness nanotechnology-related phenomena, instrumentation and machinery, whether the approach to nanoscale engineering is top-down or bottom-up or some combination of the two.

An enabling technology may be defined as "equipment and/or methodology that, alone or in combination with associated technologies, provides the means to generate giant leaps in performance and capabilities of the user" (*www.businessdirectory.com*). The case studies suggest that this feature of nanotechnology is the main driver for companies to enter the field, even though clear demonstrations of "giant leaps" in performance and capabilities due to nanotechnology-enabled products are still scarce. Further, the case studies give some insight into the different roles that small and larger companies are assuming in emerging value chains; these insights are broadly in line with the model of a nanotechnology value chain proposed by LuxResearch (see Chapter 2).

Box 3.2. Case study examples of the enabling features of nanotechnology

- The whole business idea of the company is based on the utilisation of nanotechnology. It enables the company to manufacture products which are new and have novel characteristics (for example they may be cheaper than traditional measurement or screening devices or processes).

- Nanotechnology is an enabling technology with wide potential applications in almost any area within the field of medical devices. [We] make soft tissue attachment technology for implant surfaces that prevent infections and quicken the healing process.

- The utilisation of particle technology improves efficiency in diagnostic tests: it is possible to provide more accurate and quantitative information about the properties of tested substances.

- The aim of the [nanotechnology] research is to improve electromagnetic properties of core materials and components [...] in order to lower power transmission losses and costs.

- New types of products with built-in functions and improved energy efficiency and greater robustness may be created.

- [The company] uses nanocomposites to develop, produce and market systems solutions for equipping products with new and additional functional properties.

- The acoustic mechanism [of nanodroplets] completely eliminates the need for pipette tips, pin tools or nozzles, which further eliminates the need to wash the transfer mechanism.

- [...] focuses on devices to replicate human capillary action. They automate the secondary screening and preclinical animal *in vivo* trials processes which are normally labour-intensive.

- The company has recently developed a [...] process for attaching various nano-sized materials to different types of powders. With [this process], the company is seeking a new business area including agriculture, fish farming, livestock farming and silk production.

- The company is exploring the use of nanomaterials to improve the performance of materials systems used in building cars and light trucks, including paints, plastics, metals and lubricants. Recently the company has also been studying advanced battery and fuel cell designs, presented via its supply base, which incorporate nanomaterials for improved performance.

The majority of the small companies in the sample populate the second segment of the nanotechnology value chain which supplies various intermediate products with nanoscale features (powders for cosmetics or health products, coatings for construction elements, coatings and sensors for machinery and related components, lightweight and durable materials to reduce maintenance costs, etc.). As noted above, these small companies are typically science-based and experiment with a broader range of applications than bigger companies (see Boxes 3.3 and 3.4 for examples). The majority of medium-sized companies fall into the category of developers of supporting instrumentation and sometimes have a more distant relation with nanotechnology; they may not themselves apply nanotechnology but rather provide the tools that enable other companies to do so.

Box 3.3. SouthWest NanoTechnologies Incorporated, United States

SouthWest NanoTechnologies Inc. (SWeNT) is a producer of carbon nanotubes. The company was founded in April 2001 by Professor Daniel Resasco at the University of Oklahoma, and boasts its own patented catalytic technology known as CoMo CAT. It employs 14 persons and reported USD 457 010 in sales in 2008.

The company's main product consists of Single-Wall Carbon Nanotubes (SWNTs), which are used in end-markets such as aerospace, automotive, defence, medical, solar energy, wind energy, lighting, electronics, polymer composites, displays and xerography. SWNTs exhibit unique properties due to their unusual structure. They consist of hollow cylinders of carbon of approximately 1 nm in diameter and are up to 1 000 times as long as they are wide. This structure has remarkable optical and electronic properties, tremendous strength and flexibility, and high thermal and chemical stability.

SouthWest's nanotubes are distinguished by their purity. The CoMoCAT process has been refined to grow significant amounts of SWNTs in less than one hour with a selectivity greater than 90%. The company claims to have enhanced the predictability of the nanotube's properties, including chirality. The ready scalability and intrinsic high selectivity of their production process reportedly solves the low cost-high product quality dilemma.

SWeNT's interest at the moment is to remain a first-line provider of Single-Wall NanoTubes (SWNTs). SWeNT decided to stay with their main line of business, producing SWNTs, rather than moving up the value chain (by focusing on applications for SWNTs). The main reason cited is that the number of possible applications is very broad, and that one company could not maintain leadership in all.

Box 3.4. Impact Coatings, Sweden

Impact Coatings was founded in 1997 as a spin-off from Linköping University. The company's core capability is in thin film coatings. Impact Coatings produces coatings and instruments for the production of coatings. It is a coating intermediate product and service supplier in the value chain, delivering a component input to the customer but never the component itself. Impact Coatings mainly provide coatings for electrical contacts, corrosion protection in fuel cells and batteries, plus functional and decorative coatings. The company is not part of a corporate group and it is listed on the stock exchange.

Nanotechnology activities constitute an essential part of Impact Coatings' operations. The company bases its business on the surface treatment method of PVD (Physical Vapour Deposition), in which nanotechnology is central. Impact has then developed a number of solutions that apply the method. Hence, almost all its previously presented products and services include nanotechnology features.

Impact Coatings' main end-user markets are found in electronic handsets and computers, smartcards, memory cards, fuel cells and batteries, and spectacle frames. The main geographic markets are Denmark, China and Sweden. Around 90% of Impact Coatings' markets are outside of Sweden.

Specific nanotechnology activities are found mainly in the company's operations in product and service R&D, production and manufacturing, quality control and to a smaller extent in marketing.

The larger companies mainly populate the third segment of the value chain, as identified by LuxResearch. They typically integrate intermediate products with nanoscale features into larger product systems (*e.g.* machinery, telecommunications equipment, transport and avionics, power and auto-mation systems) in their existing business lines, often in collaboration with smaller companies. In some cases nanotechnology developments represent a natural evolution of the competence base of large and established companies, electronics and semiconductors being good examples (see Box 3.5 for an example). In other cases larger companies mainly monitor developments in anticipation of possible technological discontinuities which may create new business in the longer term (see Box 3.6 for an example).

Box 3.5. EV Group, Austria

EV Group (EVG) is a world leader in wafer-processing solutions for semiconductor, MEMS and nanotechnology applications. Through close collaboration with its global customers, the company implements its flexible manufacturing model to develop reliable, high-quality, low-cost-of-ownership systems that are easily integrated into customers' fab lines. Key products include wafer bonding, lithography/nanoimprint lithography (NIL) and metrology equipment, as well as photoresist coaters, cleaners and inspection systems.

In addition to its dominant share of the market for wafer bonders, EVG holds a leading position in NIL and lithography for advanced packaging and MEMS. Along these lines, the company co-founded the EMC-3D consortium in 2006 to create and help drive implementation of a cost-effective through-silicon-via (TSV) process for chip packaging and MEMS/sensors. Other target semiconductor-related markets include silicon-on-insulator (SOI), compound semiconductor and silicon-based power-device solutions.

Founded in 1980, EVG is headquartered in St. Florian, Austria, and operates via a global customer support network, with subsidiaries in Tempe, AZ.; Albany, NY.; Yokohama and Fukuoka, Japan; Seoul, Korea; and Chung-Li, Chinese Taipei. Integrated R&D and all production steps at the headquarters in Austria allows EVG to respond quickly to new technology developments, apply the technology to manufacturing challenges and expedite device manufacturing in high volumes.

Box 3.6. Nokia, Finland

Nokia is a device manufacturer and service provider in mobile communications and serves consumer markets. It employed some 112 000 people at the end of 2007. Nanotechnologies are incorporated in its products through suppliers, which are again supplied by materials producers. Thus, Nokia is not directly involved in the production of components utilising nanotechnology, but currently focuses on research and development of new technologies and concepts for future products and services. Nokia started its involvement in nanotechnology through micromechanics in 1999 followed by a Nanotechnology Vision in 2004. Nokia's dedicated nanotechnology laboratory was established in 2007.

Nokia is now evaluating and developing nanotechnology-based products and services that the company would sell directly. Currently, nanotechnology is not viewed as one of its core competences, but is one of its research focus areas. It has a clear vision of the potential of nanotechnology. Nokia has launched several concept-based projects, which are aimed towards the creation of new products and potentially new businesses within 6-10 years. This also is the predicted time span in which nanotechnology will have a significant impact on the mobile communication industry (both products and services).

Nokia's nanotechnology-related R&D areas are energy solutions, functional surface materials, transparency and compliancy, integration and customisation, integrated sensors, and energy efficient computing.

Areas of activity

The emerging nature of nanotechnology is also reflected in Figure 3.5 which shows activities of case study companies that involve nanotechnology in one way or another (as one dimension of R&D or production, as part of strategic considerations relating to marketing or to environmental, health and safety [EHS] issues, imports, exports or some other activity). All interviewed companies undertake nanotechnology R&D activities, but the share declines gradually for involvement in nanotechnology at later phases of innovation and commercialisation, *i.e.* production, quality control, marketing, legal, regulatory or IP activities, or those relating to EHS, imports or exports. At the same time it is interesting to note the broad range of activities that involve nanotechnology.

Figure 3.5. Activities involving nanotechnology

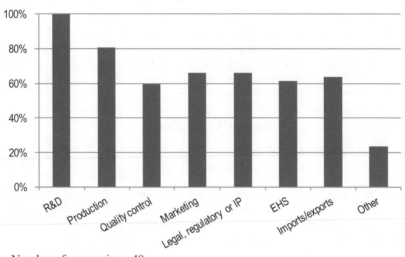

Number of companies = 48.

An analysis of nanotechnology-related activities by company size does not reveal clear differences. The only noteworthy observation concerns activities relating to legal, regulatory, IPRs or EHS issues; larger companies indicate more involvement in these activities than smaller ones. This finding is unsurprising, as larger companies tend to have legal and IP departments and better equipped R&D laboratories. They are thus better placed than smaller companies to deal with IPR and EHS issues. This finding may also reflect the involvement of larger companies in more mature nanotechnology sub-areas, so that commercialisation is further advanced, and EHS and IPR issues therefore gain in importance.

The questionnaire also asked for the share of nanotechnology activities in total sales, employees, R&D expenditures, production costs and capital spending of the company. Overall the companies had difficulty providing these figures as nanotechnology is not monitored by their accounting systems. Nanotechnology is typically only one of many fields that companies draw on during R&D and production, and they do not separate out nanotechnology employees.

Problems for providing quantitative figures on nanotechnology activities and their economic impact were greatest for the larger companies and the companies involved in nanobiotechnology. For larger companies, this finding underlines the fact that nanotechnology typically only represents one out of several technology fields which they are concerned with. For nano-biotechnology the explanation may be that the convergence of biotech-nology and nanotechnology makes it difficult to single out the economic significance of nanotechnology in any meaningful way. However, 68% of the companies defined themselves as nanotechnology-dedicated by indicating that nanotechnology forms the core of their business, and roughly 50% of these companies reported that nanotechnology accounts for 100% of their sales, employees, R&D expenditures, production costs (in so far as they are involved in production) and capital spending. These companies are typically small or medium-sized, and recently established.

Sources of competences and innovation

Universities are often mentioned as a source of competences by the case study companies, although in-house R&D is of primary importance for companies of all sizes (see Figure 3.6). On a closer look, it is evident that universities are relatively more important for smaller companies, and that larger companies tend to combine in-house R&D activities with collabora-tion across a broader range of organisations, mainly universities and govern-ment laboratories. It is worth noting that other for-profit companies do not appear as important collaborators in any company size group, despite the recent attention given to strategic alliances, partnerships and "open" modes of innovation (OECD, 2008). It may be that the science-oriented nature and early phase of nanotechnology commercialisation discourage horizontal collaboration with companies that may become competitors in markets for applications.

Figure 3.6. Sources of nanotechnology competences by company size

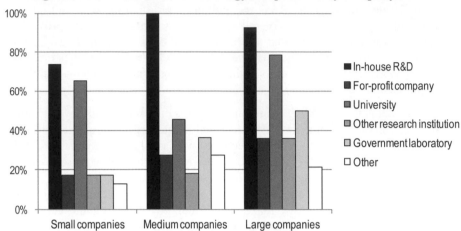

Number of companies = 48.

Box 3.7. Kibron, Finland

Kibron was established in 1994 by leading pioneers in the field of surface science, headed by Dr. Paavo Kinnunen. The company had 12 employees and total annual sales of EUR 700 000 in 2006. Drawing on nanotechnology and nanoscale phenomena, the company develops, manufactures and markets surface chemistry measuring instruments.

The technological basis of the company draws on research on biomolecules since the 1970s by Dr. Paavo Kinnunen, who is currently chair of the Board. He still holds a chair at the University of Helsinki and is able to draw on his networks of students and colleagues to commission research projects and acquire technological knowledge and know-how for the company. He is also, in his capacity of university professor, involved in international collaborative R&D projects, and through his role as a reviewer, acquires the latest research knowledge in the field. About 60% of the company's competence-building is based on collaboration with the University of Helsinki. Additionally, there is collaboration with foreign universities.

The main products of the company are: equipment for PLD screening, physic-chemical profiling, the instrumentation for surface chemistry (tensiometers), and industrial applications in drug discovery and development of surfactant-based formulations.

The company's customers are R&D labs in the pharmaceuticals industry, manufac-turers of surface tension products (such as soaps, printing ink), petrochemical industry, and university laboratories.

Interactions between universities and smaller companies take many forms. Smaller companies are generally university spin-offs and their origin can often be traced to specific research projects. Sometimes the scientists themselves are the founders of the company. In other cases the original idea is licensed from the university or the scientists and developed further in close collaboration with one or more scientists as a way to facilitate technology transfer. The case studies provide evidence to support previous studies on science and technology interactions in nanotechnology which highlight the interdisciplinary nature of nanotechnology, the intensity of these interactions, and the role of "star scientists" in technology transfer and academic entrepreneurship (see Chapter 2) (see Boxes 3.7 and 3.8).

Box 3.8. Cellix, Ireland

Cellix Ltd has developed a product for research environments which reduces the cost of clinical trials by simulating micro-capillaries for the biotechnology and pharmaceutical industries. Cellix Ltd was established in 2004 but did not become operational until March 2006. It currently employs nine persons.

Cellix Ltd is based in the Institute of Molecular Medicine on the campus of Trinity College Dublin. The company's product range falls under the North American Industry Classification System 54171 (Research and Development in the Physical, Engineering and Life Sciences), 734519 (Other Measuring and Controlling Device Manufacture) and 3345 (Navigational, Measuring, Electromedical, and Control Instruments Manufacturing).

Cellix is entirely focused on devices to replicate human capillary action. Products include the Mirus Nanopump series and the Vena Biochip series. The target market is pharmaceutical and biotechnology companies involved in clinical trials and academic researchers in the life sciences. Cellix products automate the secondary screening and preclinical animal *in vivo* trial processes which are normally labour-intensive. The final step in drug approval is human clinical trials, where Cellix's platform is also being investigated as a screening tool for Phase I patient samples.

Understanding nanofluidics is the key competence of the company. Most of the workforce is currently from a technology background (physics PhDs and MScs) though it is expected that employees will be active across the operation, including sales and marketing. The key IP was created in Trinity College Dublin's Physics Department. The discovery and subsequent creation of this IP led to the creation of Cellix. The IP was then matched to the pharmaceutical industry's need to reduce the cost of clinical trials.

Cellix has investigated point-of-care systems but to date has not identified a "killer application" which would match its technology. This market is dominated by two major pharmaceuticals (Abbott and Roche).

The concept of receptor or absorptive capability also plays a role in collaboration between larger R&D-capable companies, universities and government laboratories. Absorptive capabilities allow companies to align their in-house R&D with externally acquired knowledge (Cohen and Levinthal, 1990). This may require gatekeepers at the interface between scientific and more applied research and production or marketing activities who can mitigate some of the difficulties for transferring nanotechnology from academia to industry highlighted by existing studies (Cohen and Levinthal, 1990). These include the basic research orientation of the relevant scientific fields, the identification of commercially viable projects, and university researchers' lack of business skills (see Chapter 3). Absorptive capabilities may also be affected by the composition of technologies that companies possess, and their abilities to create synergies across these technologies.

Absorptive capabilities can be especially important for larger and established companies in traditional industries as they approach emerging and science-based technologies. The case studies also provide snapshots of how such companies have built their absorptive capabilities over time. In many cases involvement in nanotechnology merely represents an incremental development in the knowledge base of large companies, an extension of traditional manufacturing technologies, or enhancements of existing materials. Some of the large companies have set up dedicated nanotechnology laboratories or programmes. Others depend on long-standing R&D partnerships with universities, government laboratories or other research institutions and supplier companies. Boxes 3.9 and 3.10 provide two examples of established companies, world leaders in their respective fields, which have become involved in nanotechnology in the course of the organic development of their business areas.

The case studies do not bear out the model of company dynamics which suggests that smaller companies may be the main carriers of emerging technologies, at least initially. Instead it seems that large companies may be quite well placed to assimilate nanotechnology as they have been involved in related technologies for a very long time (see Chapter 2). Previous studies also note their greater facility for acquiring and operating the expensive instrumentation, machinery and equipment needed for nanoscale engineering. Nonetheless, it is difficult to make definitive statements about company dynamics in nanotechnology in these early days. Nanotechnology is a multifaceted field and may generate both incremental and discontinuous innovation and thus affect companies in numerous ways.

Box 3.9. ABB, Sweden

ABB is a large international corporate group engaged in power and automation technologies. The ABB group of companies, with AB as the parent company, employs around 110 000 people and operates in around 100 countries. ABB was established in 1913 and the company dates from the end of the nineteenth century.

ABB has been involved in nanotechnology activities more or less since its establishment, given that material science has always been a core capability. However, the company started referring to its activities as nanotechnology activities around 1998-99, and in 2000 ABB started its nanotechnology programme. Its initial competence was developed in house through own R&D activities and through collaboration with academia and other firms. As the need has grown, the focus has turned mainly towards university competence and capability development through co-operation with suppliers. Nanotechnology is now an integrated part of the materials reserearch programme of ABB.

The company identified big opportunities in the area; consequently, the programme aims at scouting for nanotechnology activities that could be of interest to the company. Main areas of interest have been technology in early development phases within electrical engineering, nanocoatings and nanosensors.

Box 3.10. Carl Zeiss, Germany

Carl Zeiss was founded in 1846. It offers products and services for biomedical research and medical technology, systems solutions for the semiconductor, automotive and mechanical engineering industries, and consumer goods such as camera lenses, binoculars and eyeglasses.

The nanotechnology-related activities at Carl Zeiss are mainly performed in the business unit Carl Zeiss SMT AG, which deals mainly with semiconductor technology such as lithography, imaging and process control solutions. Carl Zeiss SMT AG was established in 2001 and uses the brand "Enabling the Nano-Age World".

Their optical systems have been a key element in the fabrication and miniaturisation of micro-chips since the beginning of optical lithography. They pave the way for chip manufacturers around the globe, enabling more innovative chip designs and higher productivity.

Carl Zeiss NTS GmbH, a subsidiary of Carl Zeiss SMT, manufactures a comprehensive range of electron microscopes including field emission and variable pressure scanning electron microscopes as well as energy filtering transmission electron microscopes and combined electron and focused ion-beam systems. Recently the helium ion microscope Orion® Plus has been added to the portfolio and offers structural and compositional analysis in addition to sub-nanometre resolution imaging. This broad range of nano-imaging systems offers unique capabilities for material science, semiconductor and biological applications.

Challenges for the commercialisation of nanotechnology

The third and fourth parts of the company case study questionnaire addressed challenges in the areas of R&D, human and financial resources, intellectual property (IP) strategies, value chains and production, marketing, environment, EHS, and other regulatory issues. As the main objective of the project was to identify specific challenges for the commercialisation of nanotechnology which may warrant new policy responses, case study analysts were encouraged to be particularly alert to such challenges. Challenges mentioned by companies and highlighted by the case study analysts are grouped according to the areas covered by the questionnaire.

Figure 3.7 displays the breakdown of the challenges identified by the companies and highlighted by the case study analysts.[3] Challenges relating to R&D and EHS issues are, by a slight margin, most often reported, followed by human resource issues, financial resources and issues relating to production. A breakdown of these results by company size suggests that challenges relating in particular to human resources and EHS issues affect all case study companies. Challenges relating to production are mentioned somewhat more frequently by larger companies, and R&D and financial resources by smaller companies. Challenges relating to IPRs, value chains, marketing and other regulatory issues show less variability across company size. In terms of sub-areas, challenges relating to R&D rate high in nano-biotechnology and nanoelectronics. This may point to technical complexities and barriers in these areas (technical complexities and barriers are discussed further below). There is less variation across sub-areas with respect to all other challenges covered by the interviews (Figures 3.8 and 3.9).

The point at which companies entered the field may also affect the findings. In this context, the only noteworthy variation is found for challenges relating to human resources, production and EHS issues. Companies that entered the field between five and ten years previously face greater challenges for human resources and production, while newcomers and more established companies do so for EHS issues. These differences may reflect companies' lifecycle rather than specific nanotechnology issues, given that expanding companies typically experience barriers to growth in terms of their ability to employ specialised personnel and expand production after the prototype phase. EHS issues seem especially challenging for larger companies which have progressed further in commercialisation (EHS issues are discussed further below).

Figure 3.7. Areas in which companies see a significant challenge for commercialisation

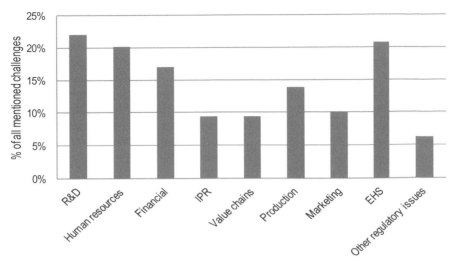

Number of challenges mentioned = 159.

Figure 3.8. Areas in which companies see a significant challenge for commercialisation by company size

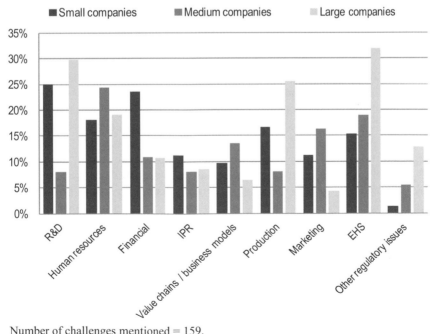

Number of challenges mentioned = 159.

Figure 3.9. Areas in which companies see a significant challenge for commercialisation by company size

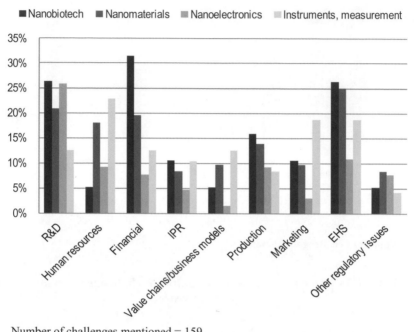

Number of challenges mentioned = 159.

Research and development (R&D)

All of these case study companies are R&D-intensive and take a positive view of increasing their nanotechnology research and process and product development efforts during the next five years. However, exact figures on future R&D investments could not be obtained, and the economic crisis may also have changed their strategies. The overwhelming majority (88%) have used government policies or programmes to support their R&D; the share is only slightly lower for larger companies than for smaller ones. Some of the latter report zero or very low sales figures which may make government support crucial. These companies are still primarily at an early stage in the development of nanotechnology for commercial applications and do not yet have any return on their R&D investments.

Box 3.11. Case study examples of R&D-related challenges

- The central R&D challenges that […] meets are related to finding analytical methods and capabilities in order to measure, characterise and steer nanoscale production processes. This is mainly connected to the absence of human capital capable of working specifically at the nanoscale.

- To go from the R&D phase to the production phase always requires a pilot phase which means more investment will be needed. [The company has] no strategy at this stage.

- […] faces internal challenges due to the length of nanotechnology-related projects. This requires patience from internal decision makers and sustained interest and funding for the projects.

- Access to timely and affordable characterisation facilities is a problem across all industries working in nanotechnology R&D, specifically access to TEM but all techniques to some extent as large capital expenditure is required for TEM/SEM (transmission electron microscope/scanning electron microscope) facilities.

- The main challenge when conducting nanotechnology R&D has been obtaining materials that meet needed property requirements. More specifically, it is hard to find materials with the required non-agglomeration properties at feasible prices.

- The challenge in designing new materials to yield specific performance properties is that even for quaternary structures (*i.e.* four different elements) only about 1% of all compounds have been studied.

- R&D is also related to biotechnologies and cognitive systems. Integration of all of these is a challenge, but acquiring new knowledge and skills in biotechnology has been especially difficult.

- One problem […] encountered in human resources is that it is hard to find qualified R&D personnel with a solid background in optics and not just nanotechnology.

- The key challenge is finding the same language (*e.g.* terminology and use of different methods). [The] know-how about converging theoretical and applied research is most useful.

- The main R&D challenge is differentiating between useful nanotechnology research focused on solving industry issues and esoteric university nanotechnology research. Establishing useful collaborations has also proved problematic because academics have different drivers from industry, *e.g.* academics' desire to publish research is inconsistent with XXX protecting trade secrets.

- A nanotechnology-specific aspect of the R&D challenges is arguably the sheer extent of potential applications: identifying customers therefore requires research.

Challenges relating to R&D typically concern the present complex and immature nature of nanotechnology, which creates technological barriers for application and commercialisation (see Box 3.11). The case studies suggest that the companies have a relatively good understanding of nanotechnology under laboratory conditions, but that scalability of related manufacturing processes for prototype and industrial production introduces significant hurdles. The specific barriers vary across nanotechnology sub-areas and application fields, as well as by the position of the company in the value chain. For example, one large company mentioned the poor reproducibility of nanotechnology-enabled products when manufactured in greater quantities owing to unresolved technological issues. Another large company attributed poor process scalability to the absence of methodologies for measuring, characterising and steering nanoscale manufacturing processes and pointed to the need for technological standards to safeguard the quality of manufactured nanostructures. Such issues can raise costs and prolong R&D projects.

More generally, the company case studies point to a close relation between nanoscale manufacturing processes and product innovation, *i.e.* the development of new products, or new functionalities and properties for existing products. As a consequence, new product development requires the development of relevant nanoscale manufacturing processes to the point where prototype and industrial-scale production becomes viable and manageable. Manufacturing bottlenecks may thus have direct and negative effects on R&D activities further upstream. As Box 3.11 shows, larger companies highlight quality problems with nanomaterials when these are required in larger quantities from suppliers. Conversely, a small company noted difficulties in combining R&D with high-volume production. Others mentioned the lack, or high cost, of instrumentation related to EHS research and testing which also affects manufacturing. All of these examples support the main findings of company surveys referred to in Chapter 3.

As the examples in Box 3.11 suggest, some R&D challenges are also directly related to the lack of relevant human resources. For example, one company stressed the need for employees with specific nanotechnology skills as (nanotechnology-related) manufacturing processes become more advanced. Others noted that new instrumentation and the close relations between nanotechnology, biotechnology and other advanced technologies may require retraining or the hiring of new personnel. A large ICT company called attention to the relations between nanotechnology and biotechnologies, as well as cognitive sciences (the convergence between these fields is often referred to as "NBIC") as an R&D challenge. This type of cross-pollination, even convergence, between various sciences and technologies may be a primary reason why R&D-related challenges seem to be more pronounced in nanobiotechnology and nanoelectronics. However, technological skills are not always enough. Communication skills ("finding the same language") also become increasingly important for facilitating collaboration with scientists and engineers from various disciplines.

Finally, university-industry collaboration was also mentioned as a challenge. The interviewed companies sometimes find it difficult to identify commercially relevant university research, and interdisciplinary collaboration may be further complicated if it also spans organisational borders. University researchers are typically driven by different incentives (reputation, publications) from those of companies (royalties, proprietary patents). These clashes of incentives may be accentuated in the case of nanotechnology as an emerging field at the forefront of scientific research, where the race to publish new discoveries is especially intense. The case study findings are also largely in line with previous studies on the transfer of nanotechnology from university to industry (see Chapter 2).

Human resources

The questionnaire asked companies to rank their anticipated human resource needs over the next five years by main areas of activity as well as the difficulties they experience in hiring employees for these activities. Figure 3.10 presents the average rankings for both of these questions. As expected, the highest anticipated need for human resources relates to R&D, followed by production, quality control, marketing and other activities that support commercialisation more directly. Small companies anticipate more growth in demand for R&D- and production-related human resources than larger companies. In other respects, company size and nanotechnology sub-area do not play a noteworthy role in the responses. Further, the distribution of the difficulties that companies experience in hiring employees across activities is very similar to the distribution of anticipated growth in human resources across these same activities.

The anticipated higher need for, and difficulties in, recruiting human resources for activities relating to R&D and production, especially among small companies, reinforces the impression that R&D and production activities are related and that both are important for commercialisation. Nanoscale manufacturing processes are R&D-intensive, complex and demanding, especially when moving from laboratory conditions towards prototype and industrial-scale production. Costs also play a role, as the acquisition of relevant instrumentation, machinery and equipment is expensive and their operation and maintenance may require dedicated human resources.

Figure 3.10. Anticipated growth in human resource needs and difficulties in hiring these by area of company activity

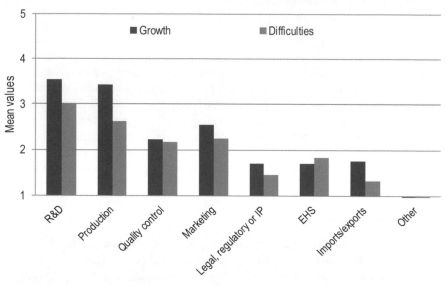

Number of companies = 47.
Mean values on a scale from 1 = no new hiring and 5 = highest growth respectively,
1 = no difficulty and 5 = significant difficulty.

Apart from these general observations, the case study template highlights some specific human resource challenges, as described in Box 3.12. Nanotechnology involves specialised skills which some companies feel are in short supply in their country. The combination of these skills in inter-disciplinary collaboration also seems to be of concern. While these companies require employees with highly specialised skills, they also require generalists with the skills to work across multiple fields, operate laboratories and co-ordinate R&D projects. Such generalists can act as gatekeepers not only in relation to collaboration with universities and other external organisations but also within the company. A PhD degree may often not be a requirement in this case; nanotechnology companies also need to tap into the market for technicians, engineers and others with more practical skills. These finding are in accord with the study by Singh (2007) referred to in Chapter 2.

Box 3.12. Case study examples of challenges relating to human resources

- [There are] some problems in finding personnel with skills at the interface between material science and electrical engineering, as well as in surface science, in the understanding of compounding mechanisms, and in the scaling up of nanotechnology-related applications.

- There is a need for very skilled persons along the value chain from growth of crystals to the final product. Very modern equipment is used and high skills are needed.

- Owing to the interdisciplinary character of the […] activities and the fast-evolving sector at the interface of nanotechnology and life sciences, it is a challenge to have enough good co-workers. As important is teamwork ability and market-driven science knowledge. Hence the need for in-house training is evident.

- An important competence and central element of the […] culture is to bring together interdisciplinary competences and think in terms of customers´ products.

- […] described its HR issues as being related to the hiring of "generalists", that is, the employees who run the laboratories, who are the basic operating technicians, etc. It does not have a problem in hiring specialist engineers.

- The company has developed a particular competence in integrating employees from different scientific disciplines, a frequent challenge for nanotechnology firms.

- Recruiting highly skilled nanoscale scientists and engineers who have the appropriate expertise to fit its specific nanotechnology applications is another key challenge.

- Finding qualified personnel with prior experience in nanotechnology and industrial practices appears to be problematic as well. Therefore, the source of much of […]'s knowledge base was reported to be from in-house training, domestic contracting, and university and company partnerships.

In addition, a few companies noted the difficulty of finding qualified human resources with prior experience in nanotechnology, and especially in nanoscale manufacturing. This observation relates directly to challenges in process scalability (discussed above). At the present stage of nanotechnology developments, there is little theoretical knowledge about and practical experience of nanoscale manufacturing. Companies therefore emphasised the importance of in-house training and longer-term partnerships with universities, as these can contribute to their absorptive capabilities with respect to nanotechnology. Large companies have an advantage for organising these types of activities.

The questionnaire asked about the importance assigned to different sources of nanotechnology-related skills on a quantitative scale (Figure 3.11). The importance of in-house training stands out as the main source of skills, along with university recruiting and partnerships. Overall, the importance accorded to universities is in line with the science-based nature of many nanotechnology sub-areas found by studies discussed earlier in this report (see Chapter 2). When the figures are analysed for *company size* the only noteworthy differences concern company partnerships, mergers and acquisitions (M&A), and foreign facilities. Partnerships are somewhat more important sources of skills for the smaller companies, perhaps since they often collaborate with larger companies in defining their applications. M&A and foreign facilities are more important for larger companies.

Figure 3.11. Sources of needed nanotechnology skills

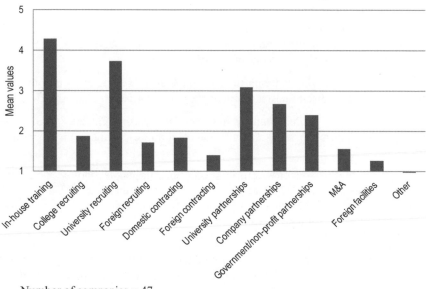

Number of companies = 47.
Mean values on a scale from 1 = not important and 5 = very important.

Finally, the case studies give some indication that human resource challenges are making companies more dependent on recruiting personnel from abroad. Already, 50% of the case study companies now utilise foreign sources to hire new personnel, and 48% are considering doing so in the next five years. The dependence on foreign personnel is common among large multinational companies with global operations. However, for smaller companies domestic human resource constraints may create impediments to growth. The availability of foreign recruits naturally also depends on legal issues (for example immigration laws, work permit regulations, tax schemes), the competitiveness of universities, and the overall attractiveness of the country as a location for R&D activities.

Financial resources

The case study companies draw on a range of sources of funding for their nanotechnology-related activities and no particular source appears to dominate. For obvious reasons larger companies stress somewhat more the importance of in-house sources. Amongst smaller companies, venture capital (VC) funding appears to be equally important to most other sources (traditional bank loans, business angels, private equity, initial private offerings, government, international programme such as the EU Framework Programmes, customers). Although firm conclusions cannot be drawn, it may be somewhat surprising that VC funding does not stand out as a particularly important source for smaller companies, given the role it has played for start-ups in ICT and biotechnology.

The findings on VC funding are difficult to interpret, especially in light of the economic crisis. A nanotechnology-dedicated VC industry may not yet have emerged. Challenges in the scalability of manufacturing processes may also scare off VC investors that seek high and quick returns. From this viewpoint, nanotechnology differs from software technologies, for example. These technologies are easily scalable once successfully developed, and have readily attracted risk investments. For companies involved in nanobio-technology applications for pharmaceuticals, uncertain and lengthy product testing and approval processes can introduce additional complications. VC investors may not have sufficient knowledge about the specificities of nanotechnology and its opportunities, and the economic value of nano-technology is hard to estimate. Box 3.13 gives examples of some of these challenges.

The frequent mention by smaller companies of challenges relating to financial resources often concerns the general problems of securing funding during the start-up phases of science-based entrepreneurship rather than nanotechnology specifically. However, in so far as start-up companies take the lead in commercialising nanotechnology, this may represent a significant barrier (which the economic crisis may exacerbate). Further, the magnitude of challenges for securing funding may be greater for nanotechnology than for other fields owing to issues of process scalability, uncertain regulatory environments and public perception of EHS issues (see below).

Box 3.13. Case study examples of challenges related to financial resources

- It is hard for companies to find funding in the start-up phase. Even though this is a general observation, not specific to nanotechnology firms, it is highly relevant since many nanotechnology firms today are small high-technology companies in the start-up phase.

- The main challenges of the company are not very nano-specific, but more general challenges that are typical of high-technology start-ups. Many of these are related to the circumstances of the country of location.

- Gaining funding from venture capital firms has been very difficult. […] believes that venture capital firms have been "burned" in the past by nanotechnology companies offering great potential but never commercialising any products.

- Venture capital is not considered an adequate source of funding. This is a very clear strategic decision of XXX that is due to the fact that investors judge the development of a new product from their economic point of view. Technical issues in nanotechnology require mostly long-term developments and not short-term solutions as is expected from the capital market. Governmental programmes should address this issue more specifically.

- The application of nanotechnology to a biotechnology-related area perhaps increases the difficulties technologically and in terms of funding, because in many application areas, the product approval processes are quite heavy owing to more general regulatory issues.

- There is also a lack of capability among public research funding actors to focus on this area. This situation hinders conducting large-scale high-risk R&D projects.

- Technical issues in nanotechnology require mostly long-term developments and not the short-term solutions expected on the capital market.

- With respect to its in-house R&D activity, the company points out that the initial investment costs are very high and sometimes hard to justify to its corporate headquarters

- To go from R& D phase to production phase always means going through a pilot phase which means more investment will be needed. No strategy at this stage.

- […] feels that another financial issue is the current concerns with how […] agencies will regulate nanoparticle-based drugs.

The questionnaire asked interviewees to rank the importance of funding by nanotechnology-related activities (Figure 3.12). R&D and production activities rank highest followed by quality control, marketing, legal, regulatory and social as well as EHS issues. This ranking is very similar for companies of all sizes. These findings are again in line with the above observations on challenges relating to R&D and its link with production, the early phase of nanotechnology commercialisation, and the specific challenges that new entrants face in this field.

Figure 3.12. Importance of funding by company activity

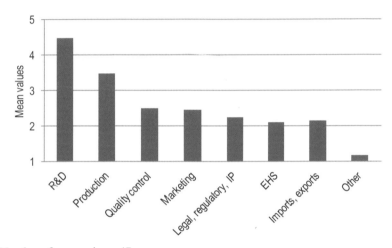

Number of companies = 47.
Mean values on a scale from 1 = least important to 5 = most important.

Intellectual property rights

Even though a majority of companies have patented their inventions, 83% also report that they use various other means of IPR protection for appropriating their innovation activities. Further, only a few note IPR challenges specific to nanotechnology despite the attention that IPR issues have received in previous studies (see Chapter 2). These findings are relatively balanced across company size and nanotechnology sub-area, although large companies patent more than smaller ones. The early phase of nanotechnology commercialisation may be one explanation; companies may not yet have been exposed to legal battles over their IPRs or they may not have developed detailed business plans or IP and licensing strategies.

The challenges relating to patenting mainly concern difficulties for articulating specific and measurable properties of the inventions for drafting patent documents (Box 3.14). Because nanotechnology applications can be hard to copy or reverse-engineer, patents may not yet be a cost-efficient way to protect IPRs; secrecy and other means may be sufficient or even preferable. Most examples reflect uncertainties regarding which types of IP strategies would be most efficient, whether nanotechnology may lead to different strategies than those in ICT or biotechnology, and whether patents will be conducive or constraining for innovation and the diffusion of nano-technology.

Box 3.14. Case study examples of challenges related to IPRs

- Since nanotechnology processes are hard to copy or reverse-engineer, a company may lose more by patenting and revealing the technology than by making it an industrial secret.

- The problem of patenting is the fact that the invention has to be described properly. Therefore the company files only key patents, which are supposed to block entrance for all further developments based on the key invention.

- In nanotechnology patents it is important that the specific properties are measurable, in order to be able to defend the patent. If this is not possible, secrecy strategies are applied.

- There are no particular issues associated with nanotechnology IPR management strategies, other than the lack of expertise in patent offices. Nanotechnology IPR can also be dispersed across a range of disciplines so searching databases for previous patents and prior art can be challenging.

- The way in which nanotechnology IPR practices will evolve is still open. IPR practices in biotechnology and ICT are very different, and the position of nanotechnology is somewhere in between.

- [...] encountered difficulties with patent thickets. In particular [...] universities/ professors tend to register patents for basic processes and even handling devices which handicap R&D instead of stimulating it. The only possibility to circumvent them is to convert these patents into standards or semi-standards.

- There are a number of patent thickets around specific areas in nanotechnology, particularly for certain types of materials. As one material can be used for a variety of applications this can pose significant problems in terms of monitoring.

As Box 3.14 illustrates, some companies recognise the existence of so-called "patent thickets", or clusters of interrelated and overlapping patents. Patent thickets have been discussed in previous studies referred to in Chapter 2, although there is still only scattered empirical evidence of their occurrence in nanotechnology.

Production and value chains

The model of a nanotechnology value chain, proposed by LuxResearch and referred to in Chapter 2, provides a good basis for discussing some of the challenges that the company case studies raise in this context. These challenges concern both small and large companies, albeit from different viewpoints. The possible lack of involvement of medium-sized companies in nanotechnology may be a complicating factor.

Challenges relating to value chains and production are often interrelated and are mainly due to the poor scalability of present nanoscale manufacturing processes (see Box 3.15). This is particularly the case for small and new companies that aspire to enter established value chains with their intermediate products (powders, coatings, sensors, lightweight and durable new materials, etc.). Poor process scalability acts as an entry barrier since these companies struggle to deliver sufficient quantities of their intermediate products while maintaining quality requirements. When the barrier of poor process scalability has been overcome, some case study companies have found it hard to demonstrate the value proposition of their applications over the traditional products and materials used by systems integrators further downstream. The problem is partly also due to vested interests and fears that nanotechnology may replace traditional materials and related services, and thus erode revenues of established companies.

However, production-related issues (*e.g.* poor process scalability) are not the only challenges that companies face in terms of value chains and production. Box 3.15 also highlights other issues. As nanotechnology is an enabling technology, there is potentially a very large range of applications. It may be hard, especially for smaller companies, to select and pursue the most viable commercial applications. Once a choice has been made, market access may be a problem. Different applications may require different types of business models and adjustments to the business environment (these issues have also been raised by earlier studies, see Chapter 2). Some case study companies noted that there may be outright opposition to nanotechnology-enabled products which could replace existing products and components that are promoted by established suppliers with vested interests.

Box 3.15. Case study examples of challenges related to value chains and production

- The main challenge related to creating a business with nanotechnology concerns the need to find fast and efficient processes in order to develop production and control techniques.

- Reproducibility of nanotechnology-enabled products has often proven to be very costly and their quality hard to stabilise. This may present hindrances for proceeding to the commercialisation stage for some early phase nanotechnology applications.

- For example, manufacturing facilities must be built in clean rooms in order to avoid particles that would cause defects and deteriorate yield.

- This is a field which has many technological barriers. This means that the ability to produce nanotechnology platforms is not sufficient, and it is necessary to develop many types of assets, such as competences in software, biological substances, applications, integration, and approval processes.

- As […] provides front-end instrumentation and novel research tools, another problem for market development is the existing old-fashioned infrastructure. […]. The future product segment distribution is relatively unsure owing to the novelty of interdisciplinary application fields.

- Manufacturing and repair organisations (MROs) have their own suppliers who supply various coatings. It is difficult to introduce new technologies and to get new coatings into this long-established supply chain.

- Overall, its major marketing problem is to penetrate the supply chains of the major aerospace companies to obtain contracts. This is because its new products significantly reduce the profitable repair and overhaul business of the OEMs (original equipment manufacturers).

- It is the connecting link between the material development or production of nano formulations and the customer's products that is to be enhanced. The challenges here lie in the adoption of cost-effective and reliable procedure techniques as well as in the generation of the desired surface quality.

- Production costs of nanomaterials (due to current economies of scale): on the one hand the markets do not take off owing to high sales prices (resulting from high production costs) and on the other hand the low volumes are the cause of the high production costs. How to break through this vicious circle?

EHS issues and public perceptions

Previous studies suggest that public perceptions of nanotechnology are quite favourable at present, especially for its potential applications in health care and the environment (see Chapter 2). However, the case studies clearly show that companies remain very concerned (see Box 3.16). Their concerns primarily relate to how the public perceives EHS issues relating to possible exposure to hazardous nanoparticles. Companies tend to feel that the public is insufficiently informed about EHS issues and fear that misunderstandings may lead to over-reactions. The public may form an overall opinion of EHS hazards which does not take account of significant variation in the severity and extent of these hazards by sub-area and application field. Some of the interviewed companies stress that they take all necessary steps to analyse EHS risks before engaging in an R&D project and steer away from areas and projects that may be too risky.

Box 3.16. Case study examples of challenges relating to public perceptions and EHS concerns

- A main challenge is the difficulty of gaining understanding among the general public.

- This company is concerned about public perceptions of nanotechnology, and in light of EHS concerns, it has decided to investigate only "non-hazardous materials" which are not known to raise consumer safety concerns.

- Key issues that national or international governments or organisations need to address are the public's lack of technological knowledge about different nanotechnology methods, their specific risks and positive side effects.

- There is a need for public awareness that the benefits of nanotechnology in medicine far outweigh any risk associated with these drugs.

- […] describes getting a better grasp of EHS issues as a major challenge and is currently working with consultants and at least two government agencies on these issues.

- […] uses the term "nanotechnology" in its market communication but the company aims at a clear distinction from technologies involving "nanoparticles".

- The company is not active in certain application areas because EHS issues are not yet sufficiently resolved. At present there is a lot of uncertainty about the conditions under which nanomaterials can be used due to the lack of regulation.

.../...

Box 3.16. Case study examples of challenges relating to public perceptions and EHS concerns *(continued)*

- The company does not emphasise the term nanotechnology in its marketing. This is mainly because the technology in itself is not the main marketing argument. Marketing emphasises the novel properties of the final products.

- The potential for using nanotechnology as a positive promotional feature of products is seen as great, but a caveat is entered regarding public perceptions of nanotechnology: there is an enormous potential for negative public perceptions to affect future marketing strategies. In this context, the company sees as unhelpful public announcements from bodies with various policy agendas which it feels overstate both the potential hazards and benefits of nanomaterials.

- […] there is great uncertainty regarding regulations and the knowledge that precedes regulations. If regulations emerge late in the market formation process or are not based on solid grounds, market development will suffer since companies risk investing in areas that later may be banned.

- EHS policies provide a background which creates demand for products. However, as yet there is nothing firm and therefore there is uncertainty as to requirements.

- Clarity on regulation would be very helpful so that the risk of litigation in the future would be reduced. Environmental, health and safety policies are not specifically related to nanotechnology though the lack of policy and regulation is surprising.

- The government gives the responsibility for assessing the risk of nanotechnology to companies without making supporting functions available. In order to foster the responsible development of nanotechnology, government actors have to provide support for testing and assessing the risks, and function as a knowledgeable sounding board when handling these issues.

- EHS policy has nearly no influence on the national business of the company, but is important for international relations. The harmonisation of different regulations would be also important (European Union, United States, Asia).

Fears about public perceptions of EHS issues have led many companies to be wary of using the word "nanotechnology" in their marketing. This wariness seems more common amongst large companies. These are often in closer contact with consumers as end users owing to their position in the downstream segments of the "nanotechnology value chain". A couple of companies suggested that "nanotechnology" is too much an outdated buzzword for its own good; the clearly identifiable benefits it can provide customers should be marketed accordingly. In contrast, some smaller companies appear to find a greater promotional value in the nanolabel.

In addition to concerns about how the public perceives EHS issues, many companies expressed uncertainties about policy initiatives (and their absence) in this area. It was frequently felt that the regulatory landscape is uncertain in terms both of the future content of regulations and the timing of their implementation. As some of the examples in Box 3.16 suggest, companies call for well-founded EHS regulations, which also take into account the multifaceted nature of nanotechnology. Regulatory initiatives would also need to be developed in a timely and transparent way so that companies do not undertake expensive and long-term R&D for applications that later may be banned. If new EHS regulations were to be implemented, many of these companies call for supportive governmental activities for risk assessment, including access to related instrumentation and infrastructure. Regulatory clarity and supportive activities also imply that companies that develop instrumentation stand to gain. Some of the instruments companies indicated this as precondition for further expansion.

Finally, there is the global dimension of EHS concerns. Many companies stress the importance of international co-ordination and harmonisation of regulations. The EU REACH initiative is one example of co-ordination and harmonisation at a regional level although it is unclear to what degree it can cater for all types of new nanomaterials. There is a high level of awareness of EHS issues in the case study sample and recognition that these issues have not yet entered the public debate in earnest.

Summary

The company case study findings reported in this chapter can be summarised in the following points:

- The case studies provide examples of the enabling nature of nano-technology; this is one of the main drivers for companies to enter the field.

- Almost all companies interviewed undertake nanotechnology-related R&D activities as could be expected by the selection criteria used for the case studies, but their involvement is slightly less in later phases of commercialisation (*i.e.* production, quality control, marketing, legal, regulatory, IP or EHS activities), with some variation by company size.

- Smaller companies tend to be recently established and nanotechnology-dedicated. Larger companies in our sample blend nanotechnology with a range of other technologies and seem more focused on specific appli-cations. Larger companies typically are unable to provide exact figures on the share of nanotechnology in R&D investments, revenues and sales, and they do not separate out nanotechnology employees.

- The case study companies draw on a range of sources of nanotechnology skills. Many of the small companies are university start-ups and often rely on continued collaboration with scientists. Larger companies use their absorptive capabilities to leverage in-house R&D with the help of collaboration on a broader front. They may be better positioned to use nanotechnology for innovation in the longer term.

- The case study of companies drew attention to a range of challenges for commercialisation, some of which appear more specific to nanotechnology than others. As in previous studies, the complexities and the poor process scalability of R&D and human and financial resources emerge as the key issues. However, the case studies provide further details on these challenges and also raise new issues, in particular relating to value chains and EHS.

Notes

1. Owing to item non-responses the number of observations varies in the following figures and tables.

2. Statistical agencies use different definitions of company size cohorts. The definitions used in this report are comparable to those used by the European statistical agency Eurostat.

3. It is important to keep in mind that the identification of challenges is subject to the specific circumstances of each interview and that interviewees were not given a list of challenges from which to choose. Accordingly, the figure is only indicative and should be viewed as such.

References

Charmaz, K. (2006), *Constructing Grounded Theory: A Practical Guide Through Qualitative Analysis*. Sage Publications, London.

Cohen, W. and D. Levinthal (1990), "Absorptive Capacity: A New Perspective on Learning and Innovation", *Administrative Science Quarterly*, 35.

OECD (2008), *Open Innovation in Global Networks*. OECD, Paris.

Singh, K.A. (2007), Nanotechnology Skills and Survey – Summary of Outcomes. Nanoforum report.

Yin, R. (2008), *Case Study Research*, 4th edition, Sage Publications, London.

Annex 3.A

List of interviewed companies

> *This list only includes names of companies that have agreed to be identified.*

Company	Country of origin
EV Group	Austria
Sony DADC Austria	Austria
MiniFAB	Australia
Company X	Australia
Umicore	Belgium
Company X	Canada
Xerox Research Centre of Canada	Canada
Company X	Canada
Quantiam	Canada
Nokia	Finland
Kibron	Finland
Mobibag	Finland
Orion Diagnostica	Finland
Vivoxid	Finland
Arkema	France
JPK Instruments	Germany
Carl Zeiss	Germany
Nanogate	Germany
Audit Diagnostics	Ireland
Labcyte	Ireland
Greganna Medical Devices	Ireland

Company	Country of origin
Cellix	Ireland
NanoMaterials	Israel
Company X	Japan
Sumitomo Osaka Cement	Japan
InkTec	Korea
KPM Tech	Korea
Laseroptek	Korea
Opticis	Korea
Park Systems	Korea
Nano Polska	Poland
Company X	Poland
TopGaN	Poland
Company X	South Africa
Company X	South Africa
Impact Coatings	Sweden
Company X	Sweden
Company X	Sweden
Alpes Laser	Switzerland
Nanosurf	Switzerland
Hoffman-La Roche	Switzerland
Naneum Limited	United Kingdom
Promethean Particles	United Kingdom
GlaxoSmithKline	United Kingdom
Rolls Royce	United Kingdom
Company X	United Kingdom
South West Nanotechnologies	United States
Nantero	United States
Company X	United States
CytImmune Sciences	United States
Company X	United States

Chapter 4

Main findings, policy issues and implications

This chapter summarises the main findings from the analysis of the company cases studies. It compares them with and elaborates on insights of previous studies. It also raises policy issues based on the findings and indicates implications for the future design and implementation of public-sector activities to promote the responsible development and use of nanotechnology.

A summary of main findings drawing on previous studies

Nanotechnology is an emerging technology which is currently attracting wide-ranging attention. Almost no other field has obtained as much public investment in R&D in such a short time, and private-sector investments have also increased steadily (but have probably been affected by the current economic crisis). Consultants have predicted very large markets for nanotechnology-enabled products, and forecasts suggest that many new jobs may be created. However, there is a lack of comprehensive, internationally comparable information on how different types of companies are affected by nanotechnology, how they use it for innovation, how they acquire or develop relevant competences, as well as on the specific commercialisation challenges they face.

Previous studies on nanotechnology have focused on issues which have been discussed at length in the context of other emerging technologies (most notably biotechnology) – the sources of innovation, the impacts on companies' activities, and facilitating factors and barriers in the business environment. The company case studies referred to in this report validate some findings of previous studies, provide deeper insight into some key issues, and highlight new ones.

A better understanding of the sources of nanotechnology innovation can help policy makers when setting priorities for R&D investments and other policy initiatives. Company viewpoints on the impact of nanotechnology on their business activities should be taken into account when devising policies to support the commercialisation of nanotechnology. The case studies also raise new issues relating to the business environment. These issues are important when considering the framework conditions for innovation and commercialisation.

Previous studies on the sources of nanotechnology innovation highlight the science-based nature of nanotechnology because of its broad scientific roots, the close links between scientific and technological developments, the role of "star scientists", and the clustering of activities in the vicinity of universities and other research facilities. However, the previous studies also give examples of fields of application that are largely driven by market demand; these examples mainly relate to large companies. It has been argued, for example, that traditional materials and manufacturing industries are well placed to use nanotechnology, as the demand for new functionalities of existing materials is more clearly specified than in advanced high-technology industries such as pharmaceuticals. In the electronics industry, nanotechnology can potentially uphold "Moore's law" by facilitating regular increases in the capacity of integrated circuits, another example of the role of market demand as driver. Nanotechnology can also help to address broader socio-economic concerns such as energy shortages, accessible health care, clean water and climate change. These and other examples of demand drivers suggest that nanotechnology may best be described as a "science-based but demand-driven field".

The case studies described here confirm, and provide new evidence for, many aspects of previous studies. They illustrate the role of nanotechnology as an enabler of both process and product innovation and sometimes new services as well (*e.g.* R&D services related to instrumentation). However, it is hard to single out any immediate impact on sales and employment. Nanotechnology enables new functionalities, characteristics or performances in existing processes or products and can therefore play an important role in renewing business areas and industries. It also has the potential to enable completely new applications and may provide a platform for radical innovation and eventually the growth of new industries. In addition, the case studies suggest that sources of innovation differ in companies of different sizes. The start-ups included in the case study sample tend to draw more on the sciences in their R&D activities, collaborate mainly with universities, and depend on "star scientists" who are often also the company founders. In contrast, larger companies combine their in-house capabilities with collaboration across a broader range of external organisations.

Box 4.1. Sources of nanotechnology innovation (case study findings)

- Nanotechnology is an enabling technology and the company case studies show that this feature is a major reason for their entry into the field. Nanotechnology allows for both the improvement of existing and the development of completely new products and processes, and sometimes new services as well. Companies often experiment with multiple applications at the same time, many of which are still in the research phase.

- Nanotechnology may best be described as a "science-based and demand-driven field". While all case study companies undertake in-house R&D, collaboration with universities and "star scientists" are also important sources of innovation, especially for small companies. Larger companies appear to focus more on applications which are driven by market demand, especially in more mature nanotechnology sub-areas. They tend to collaborate with a broader range of organisations to leverage their in-house R&D.

- Nanotechnology mainly affects the R&D and production activities of the case study companies. Many of the smaller companies focus exclusively on nanotechnology, while the larger ones typically blend nanotechnology with a range of other technologies. The range of companies find it difficult to single out the share of nanotechnology in total labour costs, R&D expenditure, production costs, capital spending and sales.

Nanotechnology is, in reality, not readily classified according to available taxonomies on the sources and sectoral patterns of innovation, as the variations highlighted by the case studies demonstrate. Nanotechnology is neither an industry nor a clearly defined sector and may never become one. It is currently in an early science-based phase of development, it spans a broad range of sciences and technologies, and many applications are still at the research stage. For example, the sources of innovation in nano-biotechnology may be similar to those of biopharmaceuticals, also a science-based sector. Nanomaterials may depend more on market demand in traditional industries. Technical standards can be a key source of innovation in nanoelectronics.

The role played by different companies in terms of R&D, production and commercialisation in this field is also still unclear. The science-based nature of start-up companies may determine their position in the upstream segments of value chains where R&D is the most important activity. The larger companies mainly populate segments further downstream and are better positioned than smaller companies to align nanotechnology-enabled products with market demand and consumer needs.

Previous studies on the impact of nanotechnologies on companies have been influenced by models of company dynamics and the lifecycle of emerging technologies. It is commonly thought that smaller start-up companies are more quickly able to adapt to emerging and disruptive technologies and therefore often take the lead, while larger and established companies are initially disadvantaged and only gradually overtake new entrants as the technology matures. When technological change is more incremental, larger companies are better placed from the start owing to their absorptive capabilities and critical mass in both R&D and production. Previous studies also point to the importance of physical capital, in the form of instrumentation (*e.g.* microscopy) and machinery. Nanoscale engineering could therefore be expected to favour large and established companies. Beyond these insights, little is yet known about how company dynamics in nanotechnology will unfold.

The case studies provide a cross-sectional snapshot of company activities in nanotechnology in its early stage of development. The sample is not representative of the whole population of involved companies. Strong statements about the role of small and larger companies in the development and commercialisation of nanotechnology are therefore best avoided. Most of the case study companies are small and recently established; some of the larger ones have been involved in the field for decades. The case studies also provide examples of the experimental nature of smaller companies' R&D. Larger companies seem to focus more on specific applications and often integrate intermediate products with nanoscale features into larger product systems in their existing business lines. In some cases nanotechnology represents a natural evolution of their competence base, *e.g.* in nano-electronics and the IT industry. In other cases these companies merely monitor nanotechnology developments at some distance in anticipation of possible breakthroughs. Taken together, previous studies and the current case studies suggest that larger companies are well placed to assimilate nanotechnology and can act as lead users in its commercialisation.

The way in which company dynamics will unfold and nanotechnology will diffuse throughout economies will depend primarily on how companies and policy tackle commercialisation challenges. The findings of the case studies in this respect are strikingly similar to those of previous studies and provide further details in some areas. Company surveys highlight the complexity of nanoscale R&D, its current poor process scalability during the transition from R&D to prototype and industrial scale production, bottlenecks in human resources, as well as funding issues. The complexity and poor process scalability of R&D feature strongly the case studies as a typical feature of nanotechnology in its current phase of development. The key reasons are the interdisciplinary, convergent and immature nature of many nanotechnology sub-areas, which complicates the organisation of R&D, the recruitment of relevant human resources, and the transition from R&D to pilot and industrial scale production. Poor process scalability is a greater challenge for smaller companies that tend to experiment with a broader range of applications; while larger companies have problems acquiring sufficient quantities of high-quality intermediate products with nanoscale features. The lack of standards, uncertainty about environmental, health and safety (EHS) regulations, and the lack of the necessary instrumentation are also often mentioned as issues which have received less coverage in previous studies.

The case studies also provide further details about human resource issues by highlighting the importance of specialists and generalists (*e.g.* technicians) who can co-ordinate R&D, act as gatekeepers across scientific and engineering disciplines, and operate laboratories (Cohen and Levinthal, 1990). Companies are finding it hard to identify and recruit engineers with specialised knowledge and skills in nanotechnology-related areas, and they frequently rely on foreign employees. In addition, the management of interdisciplinary teams is difficult from the viewpoint of integrating, and making commercial use of, different strands of knowledge. The literature on the organisation of R&D has highlighted similar issues in other fields, but such challenges are probably greater in nanotechnology owing to its broad scientific roots and multiple engineering approaches (both top-down and bottom-up). Overall, the greatest growth and anticipated challenges for recruiting human resources concern R&D and production-related activities rather than activities relating more directly to commercialisation (marketing, legal and intellectual property activities, EHS, imports/exports, and others).

Box 4.2. Impacts of nanotechnology on company activities (case study findings)

- The larger companies in the sample seem well placed to assimilate nanotechnology based on their existing critical mass in R&D and production, their ability to acquire and operate expensive instrumentation and use external knowledge. This finding on the relative strength of larger companies in the early phases of nanotechnology developments runs counter to the traditional model of company dynamics and technology lifecycles.

- Nanotechnology is a complex field depending on various scientific disciplines, research/engineering approaches and advanced instrumentation. Further, many nanotechnology sub-areas are in an early, immature, phase of development. These features of nanotechnology can often create barriers to entry especially for smaller companies that have limited human and other resources. They also contribute to the poor process scalability of nanoscale engineering during the transition from R&D to pilot and industrial scale production.

- Difficulties arise for recruiting human resources, especially for R&D and production activities. The need for employees, or so-called gatekeepers, who combine specialist and general knowledge (knowledge integration) and can manage interdisciplinary teams is also a challenge.

- Challenges for funding R&D and related activities were frequently raised, especially by business start-ups. These challenges are exacerbated by the poor process scalability of R&D, which increases costs and prolongs new product development times. Uncertain regulatory environments and public perceptions of nanotechnology's environmental, health and safety (EHS) risks add further complications to the funding of R&D.

- The novelty of nanotechnology, the established interests of stakeholders, and difficulties that companies experiment in communicating the value proposition of applications to potential customers (*e.g.* other companies), complicate their entry and positioning in value chains. The challenge is greater for smaller companies that experiment with multiple applications and have to monitor many different industries and business environments.

Funding issues for commercialisation are frequently highlighted as challenges in surveys of nanotechnology companies, especially among small start-ups. The case studies also identify funding issues as a challenge for commercialisation, especially among the smaller companies in the sample, and provide some insight on specific aspects of these challenges. However, the extent to which these challenges are specific to nanotechnology or simply reflect a typical situation in science-based fields in which the need for longer-term and consistent funding for R&D is pivotal is not always clear. The magnitude of the challenges is possibly greater in nanotechnology owing to the poor process scalability of R&D, uncertain regulatory environments and public perception of perceived EHS risks. Perhaps as a result, venture capital, which often plays a strong role in emerging technologies, is not a particularly important source of funding (the case studies were undertaken prior to, or during the early phase of, the current economic crisis). This may be a barrier for the further development and commercialisation of nanotechnology, especially if small start-up companies emerge as the main actors in the shorter term.

Nanotechnology is unlikely to become a separate industry but it the increasing use of nanotechnology can affect existing value chains and will probably require new business models for commercialisation. The primary contributions on these issues are provided by consultants such as LuxResearch. The model of a nanotechnology value chain proposed by LuxResearch identified nanotechnology raw-materials producers (*e.g.* carbon nanotubes, quantum dots, fullerenes), suppliers of nanoscaled intermediate products (*e.g.* coatings, composite materials, memory and logic chips, orthopaedic materials), producers of nano-enabled end products, and developers of instrumentation. The model is useful as it highlights relations and the possible division of labour between different types of companies involved in nanotechnology. The current case studies offer further insights into, and examples of, such technological and market uncertainties from the viewpoint of small start-ups. Technical uncertainties (*e.g.* complexity, poor process scalability) are discussed above. Market uncertainties relate to the multiplicity of potential applications. This means that companies have to monitor many different types of application industries and business environments; this can be challenging, especially for small, new companies.

Although 51 case studies were undertaken, the numbers become small when divided into nanotechnology sub-areas and fields of application. It is therefore hard to assess the impacts of nanotechnology on value chains in a way that would take into account specificities in companies' business environments. Previous studies on factors and barriers in the business environment of companies in nanotechnology are also scarce, except for those that address intellectual property rights (IPR) issues and patenting as well as public perceptions. Studies on IPR issues are typically based on case studies in narrowly defined sub-areas, such as carbon nanotubes, and highlight the breadth of patent claims. Broad patent claims can create clusters of interrelated and overlapping patents ("patent thickets") which may constitute a possible entry barrier.

The possibility for companies to protect their IPR and capitalise on their R&D and other investments, is a key determinant of what is often referred to as the appropriability of innovations. Patenting as a means of IPR protection has traditionally received the most attention in the literature, but it is well known that companies also use a range of other means, such as trade secrets, product complexity, lead times, steep learning curves, preferential supplier contracts, non-disclosure agreements, etc. While a clear majority of the companies in the case study sample have patented their nanotechnology-related inventions, most also rely on other means of IPR protection. Accordingly, conditions of appropriability in nanotechnology may not currently differ from those of other technologies. However, these are early days in terms of commercialisation, and many case study companies express uncertainty about good practices in IP management, trade-offs between different means of IPR protection, and about whether patent thickets will emerge and represent an entry barrier. Nanotechnology patenting may need to be scrutinised in greater detail by patent offices to avoid the emergence of patent thickets. If patent thickets do emerge, institutional arrangements may be needed to facilitate the broadest possible use of key patents in this field, *e.g.* through standardisation or various cross-licensing schemes.

Box 4.3. Facilitating factors and barriers in the business environment of nanotechnology (case study findings)

- Intellectual property rights (IPR) may become an issue as nanotechnology matures owing to the breadth of patent claims and the possible formation of patent thickets (interrelated and overlapping patents), which may create barriers to entry for companies.

- The potentials for overreaction with regard to EHS risks, combined with regulatory uncertainties, complicates the business environment for companies. Global harmonisation of future EHS regulations is considered important.

Public perception of EHS risks from nanotechnology is a particularly significant challenge; in previous studies companies' viewpoints on this issue were not covered in any great detail. The main concerns relate to communication issues and the ways in which the public forms its ideas about nanotechnology. Previous studies suggest that the public mostly takes a positive view, especially on nanotechnology's ability to deliver applications for health care and environmental benefits. However, companies remain concerned about backlashes as nanotechnology develops and begins to enter markets in larger volumes. Most of these concerns relate to communication issues. The term "nanotechnology" covers a wide field, and exaggerated statements about both EHS risks and societal benefits tend to make sweeping and inappropriate generalisations which then colour the entire range of sub-areas and fields of application. It is therefore important to discuss EHS risks and societal benefits in their specific context and avoid generalisations that lead to misconceptions.

While companies express confidence in their awareness of EHS risks, many also call for greater clarity and transparency in the regulatory landscape and more governmental support for EHS research and for developing or accessing related instrumentation and infrastructures. The general impression emerging from the case studies is that companies take a positive view of transparent and balanced regulations that mitigate EHS risks and contribute to the responsible development and commercialisation of nanotechnology. The companies also emphasise the importance of global harmonisation of regulations in this area. These findings invite further analysis of both the real and perceived EHS risks and of how emerging regulatory frameworks affect companies' R&D and commercialisation strategies in various sub-areas, fields of application and regions of the world.

Policy issues and implications

The findings from analysis of the current case studies raise a range of policy challenges. The limitations of a case study approach should be borne in mind, however, when drawing implications, particularly regarding specific nanotechnology sub-areas and fields of application. Some of the challenges may lie outside the scope of policy, while others may only apply to certain countries and regions of the world. For example, the framework conditions for nanotechnology in less developed countries may be quite different from those in the developed countries where the current company case studies were undertaken. With these limitations in mind, the following policy issues arise:

Nanotechnology is a multifaceted technology that covers a broad range of sub-areas, fields of application and research/engineering approaches; it does not share characteristics of an industry. There are many sub-areas of nanotechnology instrumentation, nano-optics and -magnetics, nanobiotechnology, nanoelectronics and -materials, of which the two latter ones have been subject to the most patenting to date. Nanotechnology can potentially be applied in almost any industry due to its enabling nature. Nanoscale engineering may use top-down or bottom-up approaches, or some combination of these approaches, and it draws on scientific advances in physics, chemistry and biology. As a consequence, a general "nanotechnology policy" may not be appropriate. Strategies and policy instruments may have more impact if tailored to the specific sub-areas and application fields in which nanotechnology evolves, while also acknowledging the multiplicity of research/engineering approaches. For example, nanobiotechnology developments may be more science-based when compared with nanoelectronics, meaning that issues related to technology transfer, funding and academic entrepreneurship may require more attention. Bottom-up approaches to nanoscale engineering may, to a greater extent, disrupt the knowledge base of existing companies when compared with top-down approaches. Bottom-up approaches may thereby draw more attention to human-resources challenges and educational issues etc. Further, policies seeking to prioritize specific application fields should also take the dynamics and structure of the related downstream industries into account.

Large companies cannot easily single out the impacts of nanotechnology on their activities, sales and revenues. The smaller and generally newer case study companies typically indicated that nanotechnology constitutes their core technology. Nonetheless, it is not always clear which nanotechnology definition they apply and to what extent they truly operate in the 1-100 nanometre rang [the threshold used in most definitions]. Furthermore, companies which develop instrumentation may not really draw on nano-technology themselves, whereby their inclusion for example in company counts can be misleading. The problem of singling out the impacts of nanotechnology on company activities and finances is particularly clear in the case of large companies, which blend nanotechnology with a range of other technologies. Nanotechnology is an enabler for the renewal of existing, or development of new, processes and products, already based on other and more traditional technology areas. As a consequence, it is difficult to define, identify and monitor company activities in this field. New approaches to data collection or new indicators may be needed along with jointly agreed definitions of nanotechnology, which enable the collection of internationally comparable and robust statistics. Qualitative case study work will also remain important in order to monitor underlying company drivers and challenges as the field develops.

General views on the role of different types of companies in emerging technologies tend to highlight the role of start-ups, but this paradigm may not apply to nanotechnology. The argument is that small start-up companies are better placed to engage in experimental R&D in new areas compared with larger companies, since small companies are not locked into 'old' business models and technologies, and usually do not have high fixed investments in machinery and instrumentation which may become obsolete. The advantages of large companies may only become evident in later phases of the life cycle of an emerging technology, when the sources of competitive-ness shift from R&D towards production and costs. In the case of nanotechnology start-ups play an important role, but larger and established companies seem to be relatively well positioned to rapidly utilise nanotech-nologies due to their ability to acquire and operate expensive instrumenta-tion and machinery which is of critical importance to nanotechnology; and also to their broader technological knowledge customer base, which offer better possibilities to identify the most commercially viable applications.

Accordingly, even though small start-ups are more often a focus of government policies, care should be taken to also address the needs of larger and more established companies and thereby facilitate the formation of more complete value chains. Larger companies have competencies to share, especially in industries such as pharmaceuticals and electronics where nanotechnology already has been applied for quite some time. Larger companies also possess assets key to the commercialisation of nanotechnology on a larger scale (*e.g.* production capabilities, complementary technologies and suitable application fields).

Commercialisation raises many challenges. This report highlights some challenges which are relatively specific to nanotechnology. Some of them apply more to start-ups while others apply more to medium-sized or large companies. It is important to recognise that different challenges are often related. For example, those relating to R&D often also concern human resources and manufacturing issues. EHS links back into R&D strategies, and problems in securing funding may also have to do with technical barriers during R&D.

The poor process scalability of R&D, *i.e.* challenges in the transition from R&D to pilot and industrial scale production, is one of the most pervasive challenges identified in the case study sample. Poor process scalability may be linked to the early development phase of many nanotechnology sub-areas and constitutes a barrier to entry into established value chains and to the commercialisation of nanotechnology. This suggests that policy should recognise the importance of manufacturing technologies and product development, as well as supportive infrastructure (instrumentation, clean rooms, centres of excellence, etc.) to support the uptake of deserved technologies. Uses of nanotechnology-based products may require quite significant changes in existing production lines, or the development of completely new types of manufacturing processes and the concomitant machinery. Policies overly focused on promoting only nanotechnology products, and neglecting the manufacturing and process innovations required may thereby be unsuccessful. Further attention should therefore be given to the technological state and competitive strengths of manufacturing in companies and industries where nanotechnology is promoted.

Companies in this, and in previous studies, also face human resource constraints. They need to identify and recruit both specialists with particular competencies in specific nanotechnology areas, and generalists who can act as gatekeepers across scientific disciplines, organisational boundaries and various engineering approaches. The need for such gatekeepers is especially clear in nanotechnology owing to its multifaceted, broad-based nature, spanning a variety of scientific disciplines. As a consequence, the management of interdisciplinary teams and the integration of different strands of knowledge are particularly important competencies to apply, transfer and commercialise. Policy therefore should seek a suitable balance in supporting the education of both nanotechnology specialists and generalists. Different countries will face different challenges in achieving this balance and will need to consider carefully areas to prioritize. Further, policy should not only focus on higher-level education (*e.g.* PhDs) but should also include practical technical skills, vocational training and enhancing the understanding of policy makers. All these areas are important to the understanding and safe use of nanotechnology.

Challenges relating to the funding of R&D and to IPRs (*e.g.* particularly the grant of overly broad patent claims, the emergence of patent thickets) may apply to the business environment of science-based start-ups in general, but the challenges may possibly be greater in nanotechnology in so far as start-ups will play a major role in commercialisation as the field develops. However, in terms of funding, the magnitude of the challenges is probably greater in nanotechnology compared to other fields owing to the poor process scalability of R&D, uncertain regulatory environments and caution related to public attitudes to perceived EHS risks (see also below). Perhaps as a result, venture capital (VC), which often plays a strong role in emerging technologies, was not considered by the companies to be a particularly important source of funding. VC funding may remain scarce since the market value of nanotechnology products is hard to forecast, and there may be a lack of investors with competence in the field. Funding issues can constitute a barrier for the further development and commercialisation of nanotechnology, and particularly impact small start-up companies emerge. Accordingly, policies should closely monitor the availability of VC funding in this area and consider means to alleviate situations in which such funding is not sufficiently available through the market. Policy makers should also monitor possible IPR-related challenges as the field develops further.

Finally, the case study companies expressed concern about regulatory uncertainties regarding EHS issues and public perceptions of the related risks. These issues affect the types of R&D projects and business opportunities which companies pursue. The sectoral specificities and key EHS risks should be identified and better understood in order to avoid exaggerated statements about both EHS risks and societal benefits, as these may often lead to sweeping and inaccurate generalisations which colour the entire range of sub-areas and fields of applications. Policies should promote specific analysis of nanotechnology developments at the sectoral and broader level, for more balanced views on nanotechnology. Further, it should support the development of transparent, timely and tailored guidelines for assessing EHS risks to cover different types of nanotechnology sub-areas and fields of application. Such guidelines should be developed at the international level to maximise harmonisation across countries in order to provide consistency of regulation for companies or for society. Clear guidelines and regulations can also provide important incentives for innovation as well as new market openings for companies developing products, instrumentation and services.

The current company case studies, along with the earlier studies cited, provide a good basis for further analytical work on the responsible development and use of nanotechnology. The findings highlight a broad range of challenges for commercialisation of nanotechnology which could usefully be explored in greater detail and in the context of specific nanotechnology sub-areas and fields of application. Some of the challenges will become clearer once nanotechnology starts to enter markets in a more fundamental and visible way. Further policy co-ordination and better, internationally comparable, intelligence on the nanotechnology business environment are essential to unlock the full potential of nanotechnology use and application.

ORGANISATION FOR ECONOMIC CO-OPERATION AND DEVELOPMENT

The OECD is a unique forum where governments work together to address the economic, social and environmental challenges of globalisation. The OECD is also at the forefront of efforts to understand and to help governments respond to new developments and concerns, such as corporate governance, the information economy and the challenges of an ageing population. The Organisation provides a setting where governments can compare policy experiences, seek answers to common problems, identify good practice and work to co-ordinate domestic and international policies.

The OECD member countries are: Australia, Austria, Belgium, Canada, Chile, the Czech Republic, Denmark, Finland, France, Germany, Greece, Hungary, Iceland, Ireland, Israel, Italy, Japan, Korea, Luxembourg, Mexico, the Netherlands, New Zealand, Norway, Poland, Portugal, the Slovak Republic, Slovenia, Spain, Sweden, Switzerland, Turkey, the United Kingdom and the United States. The European Commission takes part in the work of the OECD.

OECD Publishing disseminates widely the results of the Organisation's statistics gathering and research on economic, social and environmental issues, as well as the conventions, guidelines and standards agreed by its members.

OECD PUBLISHING, 2, rue André-Pascal, 75775 PARIS CEDEX 16
(92 2010 09 1 P) ISBN 978-92-64-09462-8 – No. 57761 2010